First World War
and Army of Occupation
War Diary
France, Belgium and Germany

51 DIVISION
Divisional Troops
404 Field Company Royal Engineers. From Jan 1917
previously 2/2 Highland Field Company
2 May 1915 - 31 March 1918

WO95/2856/1

The Naval & Military Press Ltd
www.nmarchive.com
Published in association with The National Archives

Published by

The Naval & Military Press Ltd

Unit 10 Ridgewood Industrial Park,

Uckfield, East Sussex,

TN22 5QE England

Tel: +44 (0) 1825 749494

www.naval-military-press.com

www.nmarchive.com

This diary has been reprinted in facsimile from the original. Any imperfections are inevitably reproduced and the quality may fall short of modern type and cartographic standards.

© **Crown Copyright**
Images reproduced by permission of The National Archives, London, England, 2015.

Contents

Document type	Place/Title	Date From	Date To
Heading	WO95/2856/1 404 Field Co. R.Engineers May 1915-Mar 1919		
Heading	51st Division 404th (H' Land) Fld Coy RE May 1915-Mar 1919		
Heading	51st Division 2/2 Highland Field Coy RE Vol I		
War Diary	Bedford	02/05/1915	02/05/1915
War Diary	Havre	03/05/1915	04/05/1915
War Diary	Nerville	05/05/1915	05/05/1915
War Diary	Laleau	05/05/1915	14/05/1915
War Diary	Shazeele	14/05/1915	18/05/1915
War Diary	Lacouture	19/05/1915	30/05/1915
Heading	War Diary Of 2/2nd Highland Field Company R.E (T) From 1st June 1915 To 31st July 1915 Volume II		
War Diary	Le Touret	01/06/1915	30/06/1915
War Diary	Laventie	01/07/1915	31/07/1915
Heading	War Diary Of 2/2nd Highland Field Co. R.E (T) From 1st August 1915 To 31st August 1915 Volume III		
War Diary	Albert	01/08/1915	31/08/1915
Heading	51st Division 2/2nd Highland Field Coy R.E Vol IV Sep 1 15		
Heading	War Diary Of 2/2nd Highland Field Co. R.E. T. From 1st September 1915 To 30th September 1915		
War Diary	Albert	04/09/1915	24/09/1915
War Diary	Martinsart	24/09/1915	30/09/1915
Heading	War Diary Of 2/2nd Highland Field Co. R.E. T From 1st October 1915 To 31st October 1915 Vol V		
War Diary	Martinsart	01/10/1915	31/10/1915
Heading	War Diary Of 2/2nd Highland Field Co. R.E. (T) From November 1st 1915 To November 30th 1915		
War Diary	Martinsart	01/11/1915	30/11/1915
Heading	War Diary Of 2/2nd Highland Field Co. R.E. (T) From 1st December 1915 To 31st December 1915 Vol VII		
War Diary	Martinsart	01/12/1915	31/12/1915
Heading	War Diary 2/2nd Highland Field Co R.E. (T) Vol VIII From 1st January 1916 To 31st January 1916		
War Diary	Pierregot	02/01/1916	31/01/1916
Heading	War Diary Of 2/2nd Highland Field Co. R.E (T) From 1st February 1916 To 29th February 1916 Vol IX		
War Diary	Pierregot	01/02/1916	29/02/1916
Heading	War Diary Of 2/2nd Highland Field Co. R.E. (T) Vol X From 1st March 1916 To 31st March 1916		
War Diary		01/03/1916	20/03/1916
War Diary	Anzin	20/03/1916	30/03/1916
Heading	War Diary Of 2/2nd Highland Field Co. R.E. (T) From 1st April 1916 To 30th April 1916 Vol XI		
War Diary	Anzin	01/04/1916	29/04/1916
Heading	War Diary Of 2/2nd Highland Field Co. R.E. (T) From 1st May 1916 To 30th May 1916		
War Diary	Anzin	01/05/1916	30/05/1916

Heading	War Diary Of 2/2nd Highland Field Co. R.E (T) From 1st June 1916 To 30th June 1916 Vol 13		
War Diary		01/06/1916	30/06/1916
Heading	War Diary Of 2/2nd Highland Field Co. R.E (T) From 1st July 1916 To 31st July 1916 Vol 14		
War Diary	Mt St Eloi	01/07/1916	21/07/1916
War Diary	Becourt	22/07/1916	28/07/1916
War Diary	Fricourt	29/07/1916	31/07/1916
Heading	51st Divisional Engineers 2/2nd Highland Field Company R.E. August 1916		
War Diary	Becourt	01/08/1916	18/08/1916
War Diary	Armentieres	19/08/1916	31/08/1916
Heading	War Diary Of 2/2nd Highland Field Co. R.E. (T) From 1st September 1916 To 29th September 1916		
War Diary	Armentieres	01/09/1916	29/09/1916
Heading	War Diary Of 2/2nd Highland Field Co. R.E (T) From 1st October 1916 To 31st October 1916		
War Diary	Gezaincourt	01/10/1916	17/10/1916
War Diary	Mailly Maillet	18/10/1916	27/10/1916
War Diary	Forceville	29/10/1916	31/10/1916
Heading	War Diary Of 2/2nd Highland Field Co RE (T) From 1st Nov 1916 To 30th Nov 1916		
War Diary	Forceville	01/11/1916	23/11/1916
War Diary	Bouzincourt	27/11/1916	27/11/1916
War Diary	Ovillers Post	28/11/1916	30/11/1916
Heading	War Diary Of 2/2nd Highland Field Co. RE (T) From 1st December 1916 To 31st December 1916		
War Diary	Ovillers Post	01/12/1916	08/12/1916
War Diary	La Boiselle	09/12/1916	31/12/1916
Heading	War Diary Of 2/2nd Highland Field Co. R.E (T) From 1st January 1917 To 31st January 1917 Vol 20		
War Diary	La Boiselle	01/01/1917	11/01/1917
War Diary	Puchvillers	12/01/1917	13/01/1917
War Diary	Gezaincourt	14/01/1917	14/01/1917
War Diary	Cramont	15/01/1917	15/01/1917
War Diary	Le Titre	16/01/1917	31/01/1917
Heading	War Diary Of 404th (Highland) Field Co. R.E. (T) From 1st February 1917 To 28th February 1917		
War Diary	Le Titre	01/02/1917	14/02/1917
War Diary	Maroeuil	15/02/1917	28/02/1917
Heading	War Diary Of 404th (Highland) Field Co.R.E. (T) From 1st March 1917 To 31st March 1917 Vol 22		
War Diary	Maroeuil	01/03/1917	30/03/1917
Heading	War Diary Of 404th Highland Field Coy R.E. From 1st To 30th April 1917 Vol 23		
War Diary	Maroeuil	01/04/1917	11/04/1917
War Diary	St Nicholas	12/04/1917	12/04/1917
War Diary	Arras	13/04/1917	30/04/1917
Heading	War Diary Of 404th (Highland) Field Coy R.E (T) From 1st To 31st May 1917		
War Diary	St Nicholas (Arras)	01/05/1917	15/05/1917
War Diary	Arras	15/05/1917	31/05/1917
Heading	War Diary Of 404th (Highland) Field Coy R.E. From 1st To 30th June 1917		
War Diary	Averdoingt	01/06/1917	04/06/1917
War Diary	Conteville	05/06/1917	08/06/1917

Type	Location	Start	End
War Diary	Longuenesse	09/06/1917	09/06/1917
War Diary	Ouestmont	10/06/1917	15/06/1917
War Diary	A.29 C Central	16/06/1917	30/06/1917
Heading	War Diary Of 404th (Highland) Field Coy R.E. From 1st To 31st July 1917		
War Diary	A 29 C Central	01/07/1917	11/07/1917
War Diary	A 27 B 34	12/07/1917	31/07/1917
Heading	War Diary Of 404th (Highland) Field Coy R.E. (T) From 1st To 31st August 1917 Vol 27		
War Diary	A 27 B.3.4. Ref Map Belgium Sheet 28 N.W. 1/20000	01/08/1917	13/08/1917
War Diary	A 27 B.3.4	14/08/1917	31/08/1917
Heading	War Diary Of 404th Highland Coy R.E. From 1st To 30th September 1917		
War Diary	A 27 B 34	01/09/1917	02/09/1917
War Diary	A21 A 64	03/09/1917	30/09/1917
Heading	War Diary Of 404th (Highland) Field Coy R.E. From 1st To 31st October 1917		
War Diary	Achiet Le Petit	01/10/1917	05/10/1917
War Diary	T.1.C.7.3	06/10/1917	31/10/1917
Heading	War Diary Of 404th (Highland) Field Coy R.E. From 1st To 30th November 1917		
War Diary	Montenescourt Ref. (Lens II)	01/11/1917	17/11/1917
War Diary	Neuville Bourjonval (Ref France 57C)	18/11/1917	30/11/1917
Heading	War Diary Of 404th Highland Field Company R.E. December 1917		
War Diary	Rear HQs	01/12/1917	01/12/1917
War Diary	Neuville Bourjonval Adv HQs	02/12/1917	02/12/1917
War Diary	K.15.A.23	03/12/1917	03/12/1917
War Diary	Lebucquiere	04/12/1917	04/12/1917
War Diary	Fremicourt	05/12/1917	06/12/1917
War Diary	Beugny	07/12/1917	31/12/1917
Heading	War Diary Of 404th (High) Field Coy R.E. From 1st To 31st January 1918		
War Diary	Reugny Ref France 57c	01/01/1918	11/01/1918
War Diary	Beuny Ref France Sheet No.57 C	12/01/1918	20/01/1918
War Diary	Courcelles Le Comte (Ref. France Sheet No 570)	21/01/1918	29/01/1918
War Diary	Ritz Camp (Ref 6.9a.5.9)	30/01/1918	31/01/1918
Heading	War Diary Of 404th (High) Field Coy R.E.		
War Diary	Ritz Camp	01/02/1918	01/02/1918
War Diary	Achiet Le Grand	02/02/1918	11/02/1918
War Diary	Beuny	12/02/1918	28/02/1918
Heading	War Diary 404th Field Company R.E. March 1918		
Heading	War Diary Of 404th Highland Field Company R.E. Vol 34		
War Diary	Beuny France 57 C	01/03/1918	21/03/1918
War Diary	Lebucquiere	21/03/1918	22/03/1918
War Diary	Grevillers	23/03/1918	23/03/1918
War Diary	Miramont	24/03/1918	24/03/1918
War Diary	Forceville	25/03/1918	25/03/1918
War Diary	Souastre	26/03/1918	26/03/1918
War Diary	Neuvillette	27/03/1918	27/03/1918
War Diary	Fouquieres	29/03/1918	29/03/1918
Heading	51st Divisional Engineers War Diary 404th Highland Field Company R.E. April 1918		
Heading	War Diary Of 404th Highland Field Coy R.E. April 1918 Vol 35		

War Diary	Fouquieres (Ref. Hazebrook 5a)	01/04/1918	01/04/1918
War Diary	Camblain Chatelain	04/04/1918	04/04/1918
War Diary	Cantrainne (Ref. Hazebrook 5a)	05/04/1918	06/04/1918
War Diary	L Ecleme	09/04/1918	12/04/1918
War Diary	Busnes (Ref. France 36A)	13/04/1918	14/04/1918
War Diary	Ham En Artois (Ref. Hazebrook 5a)	15/04/1918	17/04/1918
War Diary	St Hilaire (Ref. Hazebrook 5A)	22/04/1918	22/04/1918
War Diary	Fontes (Ref France 36A)	24/04/1918	30/04/1918
Heading	War Diary For May 1918 Of The 404th (Highland) Field Company. R.E.		
War Diary	Fontes (Ref France 36A)	01/05/1918	04/05/1918
War Diary	(Ref Lens 11)	05/05/1918	05/05/1918
War Diary	Aux Reitz (Ref Marobuil Sheet)	06/05/1918	09/05/1918
War Diary	A 27 C 87 (Ref Maroeuil Sheet)	10/05/1918	17/05/1918
War Diary	Maroeuil	18/05/1918	31/05/1918
Heading	War Diary Of 404 (High) Field Coy R.E. June 1918 Vol 37		
War Diary	Maroeuil (Sheet Maroeuil)	01/06/1918	30/06/1918
Heading	Divisional Engineers 51st (Highland) Division 404th Field Co R.E. July 1918		
Heading	War Diary Of 404th Highland Field Company R.E July 1918		
War Diary	Maroeuil Ref (Maroeuil)	01/07/1918	11/07/1918
War Diary	Beugin (Ref Lens 11)	13/07/1918	16/07/1918
War Diary	Moussy (Ref Sheet Chalons)	17/07/1918	19/07/1918
War Diary	Ramponneau	20/07/1918	21/07/1918
War Diary	Ramponneau Ref (Sheet Chalons)	22/07/1918	25/07/1918
War Diary	Igny-Le-Jard	26/07/1918	31/07/1918
Heading	War Diary Of 404th Highland Field Company R.E. Vol 39 August 1918		
War Diary	Moussy (Ref. Sheet Chalons)	01/08/1918	04/08/1918
War Diary	Caucourt Ref (Lens II)	05/08/1918	18/08/1918
War Diary	Louez Ref Sheet (Lens 11)	19/08/1918	31/08/1918
Heading	War Diary Of 404 High Field Company R.E. September 1918 Vol 40		
War Diary	Anzin Ref (Lens 11)	01/09/1918	13/09/1918
War Diary	Le Pendu Camp	14/09/1918	14/09/1918
War Diary	Ref Army Map C	15/09/1918	15/09/1918
War Diary	X.25.C.4.2.	16/09/1918	22/09/1918
War Diary	Anzin (Ref Lens 11)	23/09/1918	30/09/1918
Heading	War Diary Of 404th High Field Coy R.E. For Oct 1918 Vol 41		
War Diary	Anzin (Lens 11)	01/10/1918	02/10/1918
War Diary	Bray (Lens 11)	03/10/1918	05/10/1918
War Diary	Ref France 57 C C.6.b	06/10/1918	09/10/1918
War Diary	Ref France 57 C F.15.a.4.6	10/10/1918	10/10/1918
War Diary	Ref 51.A S W T.20.d Central	11/10/1918	12/10/1918
War Diary	T.6.c.5.75	13/10/1918	13/10/1918
War Diary	T.10.d. Central	14/10/1918	18/10/1918
War Diary	Sheet 51a T.10d Central	19/10/1918	19/10/1918
War Diary	Avesnes Le Sec	20/10/1918	24/10/1918
War Diary	Douchy	25/10/1918	29/10/1918
War Diary	51.a. SW Paillencourt N.19.a.95.25	30/10/1918	31/10/1918
Heading	War Diary Of 404th High Field Coy R.E. For November 1918		
War Diary	51 A.S. W. Pallencourt N.19.a.95.25.	01/11/1918	11/11/1918

War Diary	Valenciennes 1/100,000	12/11/1918	12/11/1918
War Diary	Neuville St Remy 4.C 65.25	13/11/1918	24/11/1918
War Diary	Valenciennes 1/100,000	25/11/1918	25/11/1918
War Diary	Neuville St. Remy 4. C.65.25	26/11/1918	30/11/1918
Heading	War Diary Of 404th (H) Field Coy R.E. For December 1918		
War Diary	France Valenciennes 4.c.60.25	01/12/1918	31/12/1918
Heading	War Diary Of 404th High Field Coy R.E. For January 1919 Vol 44		
War Diary	Neuville St Remy Ref Map Valenciennes 1/100,00 4.c.65.25	01/01/1919	31/01/1919
Heading	War Diary Of 404th High Field Coy R.E. For February 1919 Vol 45		
War Diary	Houdeng Amerie Ref. Valenciennes 1/100,000 4 c 65.25	01/02/1919	28/02/1919
Heading	War Diary Of 404th (High) Field Coy R.E For March 1919 Vol 46		
War Diary	Houdeng Amerie Ref. Belgium Sheet 46	01/03/1919	20/03/1919
War Diary	Manage Ref Belgium Sheet 46	21/03/1918	31/03/1918

WO 95/2856/1

404 Field Co. R. Engineers

May 1915 - Mar. 1919

51ST DIVISION

404TH (H'LAND) FLD COY RE
MAY 1915 - MAR 1919

51ST DIVISION

121/5354

57th Division

2/2 Highland Field Coy: R.E.

        2.5. —— 30.5.15
Vol I 2.3.4 —— 22.5.15

Army Form C. 2118.

WAR DIARY
or
INTELLIGENCE SUMMARY.
(Erase heading not required.)

Instructions regarding War Diaries and Intelligence Summaries are contained in F. S. Regs., Part II. and the Staff Manual respectively. Title pages will be prepared in manuscript.

Place	Date	Hour	Summary of Events and Information	Remarks and references to Appendices
Bedford	May 2nd	12.30 a.m.	Left Bedford in Two Train loads and arrived at Southampton. Left S'hampton 4 p.m. for Havre.	
Havre	" 3	5 a.m.	Arrived Havre, went to No 5 Rest Camp. Left Rest Camp at 11.30 p.m. for Point 3, Entraining Pt.	
Havre	" 4	6 a.m.	Left Havre, travelled all day by Rouen + Dieppe to Merville.	
Merville	" 5	6 a.m.	Arrived Merville, & took the road for Roberg at 9 a.m. Parent Roberg took up quarters at Caléau	
Caléau	" 5th		Received billets at Caléau. Caired Coy in Marching Order on Coy + were at all times on Two hours notice to move.	
"	" 14	10 a.m.	Left Caléau en route for Merris, passed Merris village into billets in Stazeele near Bailleul.	
Stazeele	" 14-18		Remained billeted in Stazeele, on Two hours notice & Caired our moving. Weather broken but warm.	
"	" 18	0.30 p.m.	Left Stazeele & Vieille Chapelle, travelled all night by road. Cold night, quite a frost train.	
Laventie	" 19	5 a.m.	Arrived & got billets in Gue L. Street, along with 5th R.H.Field Coy. Situated & new but was billed & was shelled, so we stayed on. At night was conducted by Maj. Forbes 11th Fld. Coy. & Old German line, which 2 Secs. were invariably taken over the line by Two & his Subalterns. Not neglecting Heindungs, intake parade, & made new parapet	
"			Col. Rees told me to pick up two teams of his front line Lieut. Lauft himself laid this out. The enemy developed a small fire attack about 11 p.m. which kept us out in the open. Kept us constantly busy complete the line. The other Two sections were out at night neglecting & patching under Regular instructions:	
"	21		This night Lieut Lauft self conducted further reconnaissance to the front, to rectify on his sections worked up front	
"	22		Indian Inf. Minion dug this new line of Secs, wired, unrelocated, though this was a lot of flares. Mr Warres kept repairing along on Old German sump line has condition.	
			Colin McJackson, Maj. R.E.	

1577 Wt. W10791/1773 500,000 1/15 D. D. & L. A.D.S.S./Forms/C. 2118.

WAR DIARY
or
INTELLIGENCE SUMMARY

Army Form C. 2118.

Place	Date	Hour	Summary of Events and Information	Remarks and references to Appendices
Jacobus	23		Steadily settled in new Fire Tr. This night. Joined up with Gordon Brigade on our right. Sappers helped with new swelling. I began a new Com. Tr. leading from old British Fire second parl. to old German Line	
	24		Steadily carried on improving Fire Tr., my sappers so helping assisting, & also working on new Com. Tr. This new Fire Trench was shelled tonight & one man had his thigh pierced by a bullet.	
	25		Not so deep. I go round during morning & stay in afternoon leaving Sermanorio a list of shelling every evening about 10-11. But no far have touched Ten only of my men. Italy declared war on Austria this day.	
	26		Met Maj. McLeod this morning. Saw new C.R.E. Lt. Col. Spencer going to 2nd Line. Everyone absent in astonishing morning knowing about it. Germans very quiet, I was able to go over front of Old German Line. Inspired the trench pumps, bomb-guns, sundries. I saw trench leaving our bright, so this is a lot of urgent work to do.	
	27		Last night our A. trench (front line) badly shelled. Little or no work could be done. Trench or this Com. Tr. Connor did well. I went over the trench this morning with Maj. Weston left shelled, big pieces of shrapnel smashing my pipe in my pocket. New Fire Tr. needs a lot of improvement & so does new Comm. trench. day fearfully hot	
	28		Find all of A. trench last night partly blown in (1/R) partly cleared – as first 300 yds working on Com. Tr. Butler Tr. to B. line. Two other Com. Tr. started (old German on new values) from B. line to M. line. Ground very broken. Shall of our Moonlights & quicklopes.	
	29		Inverted Com. Tr. Butler Tr. to B. line. Half finished Com. Tr. from B. & R. of trimmed up West Com. Tr. Started Knougth. Very over-due only.	
	30		Owing to our trenches a new feeling no work done to-day in trenches.	

Colin McLector Maj R.E.

51st Division

12/6357

CONFIDENTIAL

War Diary.
of
2/2ⁿᵈ HIGHLAND FIELD COMPANY. R.E.(T).

from 1ˢᵗ June 1915 to. 31ˢᵗ July 1915.

(VOLUME. II.)

Original

WAR DIARY
~~INTELLIGENCE SUMMARY~~
(Erase heading not required.)

Army Form C. 2118.

Instructions regarding War Diaries and Intelligence Summaries are contained in F.S. Regs., Part II and the Staff Manual respectively. Title pages will be prepared in manuscript.

Place	Date	Hour	Summary of Events and Information	Remarks and references to Appendices
Le Touret	June 1	8 pm	Moved to this billet yesterday afternoon. Relieved 5th Wiltshires by 2/4th Middlesex turning through no available Rd. Redows 5 day changing. Were bombarding Lects 2+3 Border Cpl. Cassett Mr. Bissett improving. Corr. S. Honoured Front line. Fatigue from Black Watch.	
	2		Myself, 1 Sect, 300 off. on R.E. Transport Corr S. relieving through all four lines. Enemy blow gas maroons in ours late in starting work. Early about 2.30 was done. What was desired to as Keir -L3, L4, L6. Lieut Shepherd with 1 Sect, 300 off. proceeded a Corr S. to L4 L15. Lt. Shepherd found, started to extend a 3" anomand Elect. Cable. This was stored, but no safety hours fit. There tranches are all old German Corr. In and very wet.	
	3		Capt. Bissett, 1 Sect, 300 off. went on to work on L3, L6, L5 for an attack on our right, by 7th Dr. musts through no desig., that only about 20% of work was done. Mr. Evans, 1 Sect, 300 off. worked on L3, L4, L5, L6. They were hampered by gas. Made good progress.	
	4		Major Jackson and 300 off. worked on Comr Tunnel W3, L6, L28. About 5 am Major Jackson was wounded slightly in the head + arm and R.to field on the 5th June. Capt. Bissett took over temporary Command of the Company. Lieut Shepherd worked on L-track on Comr Tunnel L1, L4, L5. Did enemy working + party did not work.	
	5/14		Work continued regularly on Communication Trenches and Russian Saps. On night of 14th Lieut Shepherd, R.I. Drake + 2 Platoons 1/4th Royal Berkshires went to cable up their Broken A.K.5. In view of an attack on evening of 15th. Their orders are to work until red rocket announcing capture of L10 when if advisable to go on, repair some Comr. Transl from L8 to make along point +/if attack successful to push forward repair captured tranches etc.	

WAR DIARY

Army Form C. 2118.

Place	Date	Hour	Summary of Events and Information	Remarks and references to Appendices
LE TOURET	1915 15th June	6 pm	Loaded up Parker Wagons ready as Mobile R.E. Park. Detailed 2 NCO's & 16 men for 24 hours duty repairing Comn Trenches 1 & 2 when required. Smoke Shells for Brigade Headquarters & Report Centre at FESTUBERT.	
do	16 June Reinforts.		Attack on right of our position at 6pm. At 10 pm Foreman from advanced store arrived and reported Lieut Shepherd wounded. Lieut Grant sent out to take over work and relieve & bring working party in the same home. Casualties 2 NCO's & 9 men wounded. Lieut Shepherd.	
do	17 June		Attack repeated tonight. Working Party of 300 8th Argyll & Sutherlands, 2 sections R.E. had instructions to mend to No.1 Comn Trench until Message came from 7th Gordons with (two) a capture of 410 & for to dig themselves in about 100 x in front of our present line. No messages arrived - working party & Capt Grant had to retire.	
do	18th		Working party continued repairing No.1 Comn Trench & R.E. repaired trot paths into Lonsville.	
	19th		Continued about work & also in No.3 Comn Trench	
	20th		Continued as above. One sapper killed by stray bullet in No.3 Comn Trench	
	21st/22nd		Lieuts Kelli & Bathie & Balchin & 50 [men] went out on a 24 hours duty making new trench from M8.	
	23/24		Orchard preparatory to breaking down old green Breastwork down trench to front. Capt Beat & Lieut Grant reconnoitred above. At 11.30 am on 24th 4 men including 7/6 Francis were wounded by HE Shrapnel.	

Army Form C. 2118.

WAR DIARY
or
INTELLIGENCE SUMMARY.
(Erase heading not required.)

Instructions regarding War Diaries and Intelligence Summaries are contained in F. S. Regs., Part II. and the Staff Manual respectively. Title pages will be prepared in manuscript.

Place	Date	Hour	Summary of Events and Information	Remarks and references to Appendices
LETOUNET	25th/28		Continued work on Trench M/8 - Orchard during these days with all casualties.	
	29th		Got orders to hand trees part of line & backed up Palace + Pollard etc preparatory to moving.	
	30th		Got movement orders & paraded 8pm. Marched to LAVENTIE, arrived there 2am. Splendid billet all town under cover.	

1577 Wt. W10791/1773 500,000 1/15 D. D. & L. A.D.S.S./Forms/C. 2118.

Army Form C. 2118.

WAR DIARY
or
INTELLIGENCE SUMMARY.
(Erase heading not required.)

Instructions regarding War Diaries and Intelligence Summaries are contained in F. S. Regs., Part II. and the Staff Manual respectively. Title pages will be prepared in manuscript.

Place	Date	Hour	Summary of Events and Information	Remarks and references to Appendices
LAVENTIE	1915 July 1		Major Capt BISSET went round line with C.R.E. to decide on work needed.	
	2	8/am	Capt BISSET & LIEUT GRANT + 2 Section Sappers worked at night shoring up shelter under parapet of Firing Line.	
			Got orders to reconnoitre New Support Line.	
	3		Capt ROGERSON, & LIEUT GRANT started work on this at night. Continued work on above at night. Put all hands on to it in open again as enemy system of Trench shellies bad.	
	4		Formed an advanced store at end of S.E. Railway on RUE BACQUEROT	
	5		Requested to experiment with piped Rifle Rest for 153rd Brigade started making one	
	6/14		Continued work on Support trench at night. Handed over 1 Corporal & 4 men to Brigade for erecting R. C. Emplacements	
	15/8		Started working by day on Support trench when work was completed. Finished rifle rest which was examined by General Allison & General ROSS Approved got orders to fit same in Firing Line. Started strengthening both improvised battns. Made frames suitable for reinforced concrete dugouts. The Royal about the 18th owing to fracture of leg.	

Army Form C. 2118.

WAR DIARY
or
INTELLIGENCE SUMMARY.
(Erase heading not required.)

Instructions regarding War Diaries and Intelligence Summaries are contained in F. S. Regs., Part II. and the Staff Manual respectively. Title pages will be prepared in manuscript.

Place	Date	Hour	Summary of Events and Information	Remarks and references to Appendices
LAVENTIE	1916 July 19		Continued day/night work on Support Trench. One Sapper killed today during day work.	
	20		Continued work on Support Trench today but got orders to ship all work pending the handing over the line to another Division tomorrow.	
	21		Packed up ready to move. Another horse shot owing to harness galling.	
	22		Got movement order to evacuate billets before 6 pm & march via ESTAIRES - LA GORGUE - MERVILLE. Arrived new billet area 9.30 pm.	
	23/25		Rested at new billets, & got any shortage clothing & equipment obtained & included for.	
	26		Got orders to entrain at BERGUETTE 20.8[?]. Left Billets 16.30. Marched via MERVILLE - ST VENANT - BERGUETTE. Took on two horses. Left at 23.30 with Montgomeries R.E.	
	27		Arrived MERICOURT 11 am. Detrained Leeto C's + HdQ. & Marched 2 miles to BRESLE.	
	28/29		Rested at BRESLE. Did some Pontooning on Canal for practice.	
	30		Captain BISSET went to ALBERT & went out line with Captain of French Engineers. The work chiefly running.	
	31		Got movement order to travel to ALBERT arriving there 9.30 pm. Billeted in Brewery.	

121/0695.

51st Division

CONFIDENTIAL

WAR DIARY

OF

2/2nd HIGHLAND FIELD Co. R.E. (T)

FROM 1st AUGUST 1915 TO 31st AUGUST 1915.

(Volume III).

Army Form C. 2118.

WAR DIARY
or
INTELLIGENCE SUMMARY.
(Erase heading not required.)

Instructions regarding War Diaries and Intelligence Summaries are contained in F. S. Regs., Part II. and the Staff Manual respectively. Title pages will be prepared in manuscript.

Place	Date	Hour	Summary of Events and Information	Remarks and references to Appendices
ALBERT	1915 Aug 1		Cleared up billet, arranged memorandum of had water & so to give location of all battery day.	
	2		Continued cleaning billet which was very dirty.	
	3		Arranged to start work on defences of BÉCOURT + a type of River ANCRE where temporarily reformed by French Engineers.	
	4		Started work on the above form of trades had underground pits already put in by French Engineers. Went round defences of ALBERT with CRE + French Captain.	
	5		Found courtyard in ALBERT + temple suitable place for shelters + effects.	
	6		Had working party 160 of 18th Division in ALBERT defences. Found several towers included in defence scheme still available - wrote CRE asking if we could work on these.	
			Lieut. Retakalys appointed in collection at BÉCOURT by chay billed today.	
	8		this again leaves me with two officers only	
	10		Continued work in BÉCOURT, ALBERT, + RIVER ANCRE.	
	11		Went round further defences of ALBERT with CRE. Got 2 Officers & Cyclist C. Lieut DOIG + Lieut BIRNIE attached meantime	
			Continued work on River ANCRE, BÉCOURT + Defences of ALBERT	

Army Form C. 2118.

WAR DIARY
or
INTELLIGENCE SUMMARY
(Erase heading not required.)

Instructions regarding War Diaries and Intelligence Summaries are contained in F. S. Regs., Part II. and the Staff Manual respectively. Title pages will be prepared in manuscript.

Place	Date	Hour	Summary of Events and Information	Remarks and references to Appendices
ALBERT	1915 Aug 12		Riles from trenches with C.R.E. in defences of ALBERT. Got working party of 8th Royal Inniskilling Pioneer Battalion 200 men.	
	13		11 Lieut. R.G. DOYLE. joined unit from ENGLAND.	
	14/18		Continued work on dam on River ANCRE, shelter at BECOURT and defences of ALBERT	
	20		Got working parties of 8th ROYAL SCOTS (Pioneers)	
	25		Started to prepare billet & adjoining factory for wintering. Preparing drawings for stable	
	28		Started to remove R.E. stores inside cover in preparation for winter.	
	31		Continue of work as above. Making M.G. emplacement in to brick redoubt with loopholes, rails & concrete.	

M Broad Major R.E. (T.)
O.C. 2/2nd Highland Field Co. R.E.

12/7333

51st Division

2/2nd Highland Field Coy. R.E.

Vol IV

Sep/15

CONFIDENTIAL

War Diary.

of

2/2ⁿᵈ Highland Field Co. R.E.T.

From 1ˢᵗ September 1915. to 30ᵗʰ September 1915.

WAR DIARY or INTELLIGENCE SUMMARY

Place	Date	Hour	Summary of Events and Information	Remarks and references to Appendices
ALBERT	1915 Sept			
	4		Carried on work in defences of ALBERT, Dam on River ANCRE & shelters at BECOURT	
			Fixed up Major Ruth Real & asked Brigade to inspect	
	5		Fixed up Sheltes. Major R.G. Wells according to sketch sent by CRE but finds it too large & have decided to make a smaller more invisible one. Plats nightwork on Cemetery to LA BOISSELLE	
	7		Lieuts. J.R. Warren & J.R. Wilson arrive as reinforcement. Receive orders for Lieut Berry to report to 1/1st Field Co.	
	8		Continued work on defences of ALBERT. Dam of River ANCRE, shelters at BECOURT & nightwork in front. Also Lieut Doyle makes reconnaissance of undeground passages with a view to extending them so that troops may be taken underground to the defences of ALBERT. Lieut Jackson goes on 7 days leave.	
	10		Receive orders for Lieut Doyle to report to 179th Tunnelling Co. R.E. BRAY on 1 week's approx. Lieut Doyle & Sergeant Calder attend meeting at Div HQ with reference to appointments in Tunnelling Co's.	
	12			
	13		Lieut Doyle leaves. Takes up duty with 179th Tunnelling Co.	
	14		Receive orders that we have to MARTINSART on 17th inst. & handover work & billets at ALBERT to 79th Field Co. R.E. Get Reinforcement 2 N.C.O.'s 12 men for 4/2nd Field Co. — all men who had been home wounded. Exch. of Men previously with 1/2nd Highld Field Co.	

WAR DIARY
or
INTELLIGENCE SUMMARY

Army Form C.2118

Place	Date	Hour	Summary of Events and Information	Remarks and references to Appendices
ALBERT	Sept 1915 15		Requisition put up circulars. Saw at bakers works ALBERT, also requisition 50 lengths 60" tube for overhead cover in trench in ALBERT defences.	
	16		No 2 Section under Lieut WARREN takes over bomb work at MARTINSART. Start removing timber & other stores from ALBERT to MARTINSART as very few stores there.	
	17		Hand over work & billets to Major DOAN of 79th Ltd? Co & travel to MARTINSART, billets in chateau.	
	18		Start work on 2 Redps in AUTHUILLE + 90 round cartel defences of AUTHUILLE with O.C. 6th Black Watch & arrange he starts work on them and under R.E. supervision	
	20		90 round work with General CAMPBELL + C.R.E. + arrange garrison starts work on new Support trench under supervision Lieut WARREN.	
	21		Continue work on DAM on River ANCRE, Redps + defences of AUTHUILLE, Road to AUTHUILLE + Support trench.	
	22		Start night work with 1 section R.E. + 1 Company Royal Scots on new Support trench.	
	23		Lieut WARREN wounded by shrapnel at head whilst at Support trench during day. This is second time wounded.	
	24		Meeting with CRE who intends hyperbating to-day or to-morrow. Reconnaissance of	

WAR DIARY / INTELLIGENCE SUMMARY

Army Form C. 2118

Place	Date	Hour	Summary of Events and Information	Remarks and references to Appendices
MARTINSART	Sept 24		Hope to be made + new men parceled with a view to attack. Find ample parties to start working in Communn Shr [?] reliefs improving them, widening + deepening + improving exits. Find fatigues left by troops at mouth of several of them have reconnaissance of old support trench improve basis + note how our troops alter old one. Continue day work on DAM on River ANCRE, Keeps at AUTHUILLE, Road at AUTHUILLE	
	25		+ night work on Support trench. Start Gunters pits/traces for guns over [?]+ trace of advance + prepare cross-country track where AUTHUILLE - OVILLERS road cut up by trench.	
	26		Find fatigues explains + detaching lines that they in good working order. Recent order that now all available sappers will work on lining trench sides, shelters etc which are not good.	
	28		Continue work on Dam of River ANCRE, Keeps at AUTHUILLE, BLK HORSE ROAD + Saps in Firing Line + Support Line	
	30		General Harper that our "Expol Rafts Read" will good result, forward able of same to CRE for transmission to Army Workshops.	

CONFIDENTIAL

War Diary

of

2/2ⁿᵈ HIGHLAND FIELD Co. R.E.T.

from 1ˢᵗ October 1915 to 31ˢᵗ October 1915

WAR DIARY
INTELLIGENCE SUMMARY

Army Form C. 2118.

Place	Date	Hour	Summary of Events and Information	Remarks and references to Appendices
MARTINSART	Octr			
	1		Got working parties for 152nd Brigade for Support trench & fm 153rd Brigade for Roads, Keeps + Comn Trenches.	
	2		Go round trenches with Major Boothe BM 152nd Brigade & arrange that working parties improving Living Line supt day.	
	3		Arrange to make Battalions for troops in Living Line here Rams at AUTHUILLE	
	4		Review officers reinforcement - 11 found fit to B.P.R.	
	6		Lt DOYLE receives orders to proceed to ENGLAND for further instruction	
	8		Go round left sector with Brig. General ROSS warning them that no 3 section present GRANT start improving their sector of Living Line.	
	9		Carry on work on BLK HORSE Rd, KEEPS at AUTHUILLE, Comn Trenches reimprovement of Living Line	
	11		Work proceeds as usual. No 950 Sapper S Smith wounded & send whilst working at TELFORD fm 4/2nd Highd LitdB.P.R.	
	12		Support trench & dies of wounds. Sites for new shelters selected in conjunction with COs battalions in Living Line + also 2nd class the reinforced	
	14		Received draft of (two) 2 hrs belonging to 1/2nd Highland Ltd Co is mislabel	
	16		Received draft 17 men of 1/1st Highd Ltd Co to be attached until they regain them.	

WAR DIARY
OR
INTELLIGENCE SUMMARY.
(Erase heading not required.)

Army Form C. 2118.

Place	Date	Hour	Summary of Events and Information	Remarks and references to Appendices
MARTINSART	1915 October 17		Lieut Wilson Transmitted to Troops reg white marking at backing of shelters in support trench west of THIEPVAL CHATEAU.	
	18		Start working on new shelters with 10' headcover + two entrances each to hold 6 men lying or 15 men sitting. Work proceeds in two reliefs 6-12 noon + 12 noon to 6pm on 30 new shelters 12' apart in all 4 sectors.	
	20		Work proceeds on shelters in long line, BLK HORSE Rd, reserve at end of PAISLEY AV + return road. Begin the new fancy curry to falling leaves.	
	23		Continue work as above	
	24		Brig General ROSS appears to have now deemed to flood marshes at OUTHUILLE on arrête to mend up old dam + put sluice at bridge near battures.	
	26		Continue work as above.	
	29		Find one deep shelter in BISSETT TRENCH blown in through one of German windows having rolled in at doorway. CRE. pushes observers on BOUZINCOURT - ALBERT has salt flooring one change of 60th + one of 100th on top of shelter there - Result - Enemy fired about 6" but not blown in. Decision come to that with precaution to prevent anything getting inside the shelters are absolutely safe.	

WAR DIARY
INTELLIGENCE SUMMARY

Place	Date	Hour	Summary of Events and Information	Remarks and references to Appendices
MARTINSART	1915 Oct 31		Embane work on 30 Shelters, M.G. Emplacements, BLK HORSE Rd into AUTHUILLE, + dam to flood craters between THIEPVAL + HAMEL.	

CONFIDENTIAL.

WAR DIARY

of

2/2ⁿᵈ HIGHLAND FIELD Co. R.E. (T.)

from NOVEMBER 1ˢᵗ 1915 to NOVEMBER 30ᵀᴴ 1915

Vol VI

51ˢᵗ Division

12/771

Army Form C. 2118.

WAR DIARY
or
INTELLIGENCE SUMMARY.
(Erase heading not required.)

Instructions regarding War Diaries and Intelligence Summaries are contained in F. S. Regs., Part II. and the Staff Manual respectively. Title pages will be prepared in manuscript.

Place	Date	Hour	Summary of Events and Information	Remarks and references to Appendices
MARTINSART	1915 Nov. 1		Have to stop taking stores up to AUTHUILLE by day as main road seen only be used in dark. One parkier wagon breaks in his strings already injured too in dark when taking tools to dump.	
	2		Work to commence on 30 new Shelters in firing line, BLK HORSE RD, Screen for observing enemy. New + M.G. Emplacements.	
	4		Get notice that Major EVANS will call 10.30 am 6th to see about work on G Sector as they are k later due on night S/9/hm. he won't go into work.	
	6		Orders regarding petrol cancelled + get instruction to carry on as normal to G Sector	
	8		Found places at AUTHUILLE BRIDGE flood arrested.	
	10		Work carried on on Shelters in firing line, BLK HORSE Rd to AUTHUILLE, MOUND and AUTHUILLE KEEPS	
	12		Owing to bad weather several numbers to fall in, Got orders to make a large gauntly of duckwalks for F Sector which were very bad.	
	14		Carry on work as above	
	16		Major BISSET goes on leave, Lieut WARREN takes over temporary Command.	
	17		153rd Brigade relieved by 154th get no working parties for two days.	

1577 Wt. W10791/1773 500,000 1/15 D. D. & L. A.D.S.S./Forms/C. 2118.

Army Form C. 2118.

WAR DIARY
or
INTELLIGENCE SUMMARY.

(Erase heading not required.)

Instructions regarding War Diaries and Intelligence Summaries are contained in F. S. Regs., Part II. and the Staff Manual respectively. Title pages will be prepared in manuscript.

Place	Date	Hour	Summary of Events and Information	Remarks and references to Appendices
MARTINSART	1915 Nov 19		Carry on work as before. Screen at foot of ELGIN AV not thick enough so lateral down remade	
	20		Germans sent 1000 shells into PETERHEAD & damage done on new slightly below other damage trenches.	
	22		Finish several of new type shelters & get 10 more 6 in G1 & 4 in G2	
	24		Arrange to start on shelters in Support Line as front line ones finished	
	26		Carry on work as above	
	29		Got instructions from CRE to hand a day off as no working parties available owing to relief of 154 Brigade by 152nd	
	30		Carry on work as above with working parties from 152nd Brigade.	

1577 Wt.W10791/1773 500,000 1/15 D. D. & L. A.D.S.S./Forms/C. 2118.

CONFIDENTIAL.

War Diary.

of

2/2ND HIGHLAND FIELD Co. R.E.(T.)

Vol VII

from 1st December 1915. to 31st December 1915.

WAR DIARY or INTELLIGENCE SUMMARY

Army Form C. 2118.

Place	Date	Hour	Summary of Events and Information	Remarks and references to Appendices
MARTINSART	1915 December 1		2 Sections 219th Inf Coy R.E. arrive here for instructions under "Lieuts HUTTON & Lieut HILL. Carry on work on Shelters in G Section. BLK. HORSE Rd. & Keep in OUTHUILLE & repair of BURY & OBAN Avenues in F Section.	
	2		Take Officers of 219th Co round line & arrange to start them on repair of front line every bad enemy to return to G1 Section	
	3		Carry on work with 219th Co & own Company – Stopped at 1 p.m. on account of profound artillery shot – Shoot was postponed owing to bad weather	
	4		Sappers No 655 SIMPSON.T killed by snipers in morning. Working parties of sappers & others to return at 1.30 p.m – postponed bombardment takes place in afternoon	
	6		Carry on work as above & arrange with 152nd Brigade to black work on arrival. Bent Stores in front line trenches. Also site new position for 92 & 93 Battalion Hdqrs.	
	8		One section 219th Inf Co under Lieut HUTTON to taken away to do building at BOUZINCOURT	
	10		Carry on work on Shelters etc	
	14		Lt McFADYEN goes over Tramway with OC 3rd RCy Co with a view to lettering it over	
	18		Capt WESTLAND joins this unit in order to Study the work with a view to the 218th Co letting over G Section of the Line.	

WAR DIARY
or
INTELLIGENCE SUMMARY.

Army Form C. 2118.

Place	Date	Hour	Summary of Events and Information	Remarks and references to Appendices
MARTINSART	1915 Dec 22		Receive orders that 2 Sections & Headquarters move to 152nd Brigade Area & later up billets at PIERREGOT on 23rd. Other 2 Sections remain work along with details 215th who are staying on	
	23		March to PIERREGOT & later up billets	
	26		Start repairing billets in PIERREGOT, VILLERS BOCAGE, MOLLIENS aux BOIS, & Short Rubbed huts for troops arriving	
	30		152nd Brigade arrive & take up Headquarters at MOLLIENS aux BOIS	
	31		Continue work on 152nd Brigade Billets & start making latrines at MOLLIENS & VILLERS BOCAGE.	

N. Birch. Major R.E. (T.)
O.C. 2/2nd Highland Field Co. R.E.

CONFIDENTIAL

War Diary.

2/2nd HIGHLAND FIELD Co. R.E. (T)

Vol VIII

from 1st January 1916. to 31st January 1916.

Army Form C. 2118.

WAR DIARY
or
INTELLIGENCE SUMMARY.
(Erase heading not required.)

Instructions regarding War Diaries and Intelligence Summaries are contained in F.S. Regs., Part II and the Staff Manual respectively. Title pages will be prepared in manuscript.

Place	Date	Hour	Summary of Events and Information	Remarks and references to Appendices
PERREGOT	1916 Jany 2		Remainder of Company arrive fm MARTINSART. 4 Horses left unfit to move.	
	3		Arrange workshops with motor lorries vans at VILLERS BOCAGE	
	5		Receive instruction that village in 1522nd Brig Area should be ready to billet troops brought down by Jany 30. Receive searchlight equipment.	
	7		Cpl FORBES gets 3 fingers taken off at saw at VILLERS BOCAGE. Held Court of Enquiry who decide — Self Inflicted Injury (accidental).	
	10, 12, 14		No 2 Section moves to VIGNACOURT to take up duty at 32nd ARMY School. Instruction Party of 21 OR from 4/12th Highland Light Infantry. No 3 Section to VILLERS BOCAGE to be near the work.	
	17		Carry on work in VILLERS BOCAGE, PERREGOT, RUBEMPRE, VIGLIENS, MOLLIENS, MIRVAUX & raising beds & horse standings. Put all Horses through hollow foot.	
	20		Make survey of all wells & intent for 2 days will proceed for RUBEMPRE & VILLERS First Calves Hall at VILLERS intact, in coming TARRANT Huts to Cavalry Clergy Stables	
	24		Start training of Company in Drill, Pontooning, etc.	
	27		Receive instruction that the Horse transport will be coming with Poles, Hurdles & Hut Fillers	
	29		that work in Horse Standings & Beds will therefore cease	
	31		Carry on training in Drill & Pontooning.	

51

CONFIDENTIAL

WAR DIARY.

OF

2/2ND HIGHLAND FIELD Co. R.E. (T.)

Vol IX

from 1ST FEBRUARY 1916. to 29TH FEBRUARY 1916.

WAR DIARY
or
INTELLIGENCE SUMMARY.

Army Form C. 2118.

Place	Date	Hour	Summary of Events and Information	Remarks and references to Appendices
PIERREGOT	1916 FEBY 1		Carry on training in Pontoning & Drill.	
	2		Receive instructions to send plans here to CORBIE & arrange with 152nd Brigade as to billets there. Lt. HILL transferred from 1st Argyll & Sutherland Highlanders arrives & lieut. who duty.	
	4		Carry on training in Pontooning & Drill	
	5		Receive reinforcement 11 L.T.TRAE & 24 other ranks from 4/2nd Highlders Lt. T.F. R.E.	
	8		Proceed to CORBIE.	
	10		Arrange to him sawmill at CORBIE at £15 per day & regulation Poplar trees near mill.	
	12		Carry on training & win drafts in Pontooning, Smoke helmets, etc & start on Baskets for 152nd Brigade. Camp with felling picks & work on sawmill.	
	14		Carry on as above. Receive instruction to proceed (Major Bissett) to SUZANNE & take over from 30th Division	
	16		Lieut Bailie & arrange to put through 1200 men per day etc.	
	17		Major Bissett proceeds to SUZANNE to take over from 201st Field Co R.E.	
	19		Receive instructions to return to SUZANNE CORBIE as above postponed.	
	22		Receive reinforcement 1 Officer Lieut G.J. ALLAN from 4/2nd Highld Lt. T.F. Co R.E.	
	23/9		Continue training in Pontooning, Drawing etc	

CONFIDENTIAL.

WAR DIARY.

OF

2/2ND HIGHLAND FIELD Co. R.E.(T.)

Vol ~~XI~~ X

from 1st March 1916. to 31st March 1916.

Army Form C. 2118.

WAR DIARY
or
INTELLIGENCE SUMMARY.
(Erase heading not required.)

Instructions regarding War Diaries and Intelligence Summaries are contained in F.S. Regs., Part II and the Staff Manual respectively. Title pages will be prepared in manuscript.

Place	Date	Hour	Summary of Events and Information	Remarks and references to Appendices
	1916			
	MARCH 1		Moved from CORBIE to MOLLIENS AU BOIS with 152nd Brigade.	
	3		Company inspected by G.O.C. 51st (Highland) Division.	
	6		Moved from MOLLIENS au BOIS to BEAUVAL with 152nd Brigade.	
	7		O.C. + Officers went up to trenches with Officers 152nd Brigade to take over line from FRENCH TROOPS at ANZIN	
	9		Moved from BEAUVAL to BEAUDRICOURT with 152nd Brigade	
	10		Moved from BEAUDRICOURT to LOUEZ with 152nd Brigade	
	11		Moved up by sections from LOUEZ to ANZIN with Motorcars, Motorcycles, Driving Horses + other transport. Billets took at MAROEUIL. LIEUT WARREN gazetted as Captain from 4th June 1916.	
	12		Officers, sections NCO's go out line 1, 2 + 4 Sections work for Battalions in front line + 3 Sect on task A.B. under LT GRANT + LT HILL. LT RAE with infantry commence trench Battalion Kitchens. LT ALLAN with infantry working on Communication Trenches.	
	14		Carry on work as above. Battalion work consisting of new H.Q. for left and extension + revetting with left incomplete by French Troops.	
	16		Carry on work as above	
	20		Owing to change of Battalion frontage 2 sections carry on work for Battalions, working	

WAR DIARY or INTELLIGENCE SUMMARY

Army Form C. 2118.

Place	Date	Hour	Summary of Events and Information	Remarks and references to Appendices
ANZIN	March 1916 20.		1 section plant on renewals Lewis Gun Supplements + 1 section on Fad. Pl. 13.	
	22		Labyrinth pester now called M Sector. Owing to difficulty in getting enough working parties from 152nd Brigade gun up work temporarily on forts + put section to phone to improving old shooting shelters.	
	25		Carry on work as above	
	29		2/Lt BELLAN goes to course in use of anti-gas appliances	
	30		Col H.F. RUNDALL takes over command Royal Engineers 51st Highd Div, vice Col H.W. WEEKS invalided home.	

Vol XL

CONFIDENTIAL

War Diary

of

2/2nd HIGHLAND FIELD Co. R.E.(T.)

from 1st April 1916 to 30th April 1916.

Army Form C. 2118.

WAR DIARY
or
INTELLIGENCE SUMMARY.
(Erase heading not required.)

Instructions regarding War Diaries and Intelligence Summaries are contained in F.S. Regs., Part II. and the Staff Manual respectively. Title pages will be prepared in manuscript.

Place	Date	Hour	Summary of Events and Information	Remarks and references to Appendices
1916 APRIL	1	—	Continue work on Kitchens in Reserve Trenches, Dugouts in M1 & M2 Sectors & work Lewis Gun Emplacements	
ANZIN	5		Take on active defence of old craters near Chemin Crenez to be used as advance post in Fort 17 & 13 line.	
	10		Take out water supply schemes dependent on well near Kitchens providing ample supply	
	14		Infos Commando Engineers participation to G.O.C. 152nd Brigade at strength put in Craters Lewis Gun Emplacements	
	18		4 Sappers wounded by trench mortars at L.G. Emplacement near point 275.	
	20		M7 Sapper J MACKAY assembled in 18th Ohio of Toronto. Thomson had 38 years service —	
	27		Tourist to Sappers from Regimental Sergeant Major so as to see him of latest work. Received reinforcements 2 o.R. 10pm 4/12 High Land & O.R. Russo mines put up by Germans in 152nd Brig line. Take Sappers off dugouts etc	
	28		in M1 & M2 & start consolidating craters. Some Sappers wounded by bombardment of ANZIN.	
	29		Drive tunnel through to craters at Point 503 & first craters incorporated into our Role. Pled says out to craters at 277 & place 3 Lopold Plate enfilading German trenches Pit Sappers guard by C.O. at tunnel at 503.	

CONFIDENTIAL.

WAR DIARY

of

2/2ⁿᵈ HIGHLAND FIELD Co. R.E.(T.)

from 1ˢᵗ May 1916 to 30ᵗʰ May 1916.

Vol 12

Army Form C. 2118.

WAR DIARY
or
INTELLIGENCE SUMMARY.
(Erase heading not required.)

Instructions regarding War Diaries and Intelligence Summaries are contained in F. S. Regs., Part II. and the Staff Manual respectively. Title pages will be prepared in manuscript.

Place	Date	Hour	Summary of Events and Information	Remarks and references to Appendices
ANZIN	1916 MAY 1		Carry on work on Kitchen, Dugouts, Lewis Gun Emplacements & communication trench. Necessitated by mine explosions by Germans blocking part of front trench.	
	2		Receive instructions from General Rees to prepare for life of parados at 503 & build along front on new life.	
	3		Drive in 5 galleries on far side of parados 503 to a length of about 15'. Install 3 loopholed posts with Lewis Guns on new life. Got 6 men slightly gassed while driving galleries.	
	6		At 10am fire twice under life of parados & blow up far life. Ground that appeared commanded by loopholed post.	
	8		Carry on work on Kitchens, Dugouts, Lewis Gun Emplacements & emplacement for 18 pdr Gun in CHEMIN CREUX.	
	10		Send 1 NCO & Sappers to MARŒUIL in view of raid to German trenches to practice on model trenches. Connect up to 4 old mine craters by tunnels so that raiding party can get under cover near to German trenches.	
	16		Raid on German trenches opposite M1 so carried out by party 5 officers + 1 NCO & 4 Sappers 7/hr Field Co. Several dugouts bombed & 1 blown in by Capt	

WAR DIARY
or
INTELLIGENCE SUMMARY.

(Erase heading not required.)

Army Form C. 2118.

Place	Date	Hour	Summary of Events and Information	Remarks and references to Appendices
	1916 MAY			
	16		Hard mine finish. Sappers take over fort containing 20" Garrworth rel.	
	18		Receive operation order to move on 20th inst. to take over O.P. Section from 25th Div.	
	20		Operation Order of 18th inst. Cancelled. 1 Sapper killed + 2 wounded by bombardment.	
	21		New operation Order issued 152nd Brigade goes out to rest 2/2nd Highd. Field Co. takes over work in ECURIE + MAISON BLANCHE. MAISON BLANCHE with 2 sections remaining at ANZIN. 1-2 sections in dugouts at MAISON BLANCHE. Hand over M 1-2 to 1/2 H/1/2 Fd Co	
	23		Carry on work as above in Brigade Theatre, Gun Emplacements	
	29		Receive operation order that 152nd Brigade takes over + 9.O. + all O. Section + that we take over dugouts at AU RIETZ from 106 Co RE at AU RIETZ for 1 + 2 Sections + from 130 Co RE. in O Sector for 3 + 4 Sections. Headquarters, details move to MONT ST ELOY. Sections to move on night 1/2nd June + Hq. on night 2/3rd June.	
	30		Go round new position with 106 + 130 Co Commanders + go over billets at MONT ST ELOY. Arrange about Stores, workshops etc at BOIS DE BRAY.	

51

Vol 13

to 30th June 1916.

CONFIDENTIAL.

War Diary

of

2/2nd HIGHLAND FIELD Co. R.E (T)

from 1st June 1916

Army Form C. 2118.

WAR DIARY
or
INTELLIGENCE SUMMARY.
(Erase heading not required.)

Instructions regarding War Diaries and Intelligence Summaries are contained in F.S. Regs., Part II. and the Staff Manual respectively. Title pages will be prepared in manuscript.

Place	Date	Hour	Summary of Events and Information	Remarks and references to Appendices
	1916 JUNE			
	1/2		MAJOR BISSET with 1+2 Sections move into dugouts at AU RIETZ	
	2		3rd 4th Sections move into dugouts at CHATHAM	
	2/3		Arrange & commence dugouts and everts O.P's. Headquarters and finished Return interlocked move to billets at MT. ST. ELOI	
	3		Carry on dugouts and everts O.P's. continuously with working parties of 1/6th Argyll & Sutherland H's who are king loaned on fouries	
	12		1/6 A & S.H. leave and working parties become very scarce	
	16/17		R came to shown to run sapping by. 1 N.C.O. and 19 sappers taken past on embarkation of erate, arriving here find one to left flank of crater. 1 N.C.O. wounded, and 1 sapper killed shrining wring.	
	17		Carry on with dugouts and everts O.P's with working parties from Indian Cavalry Division.	
	20			
	24		1 N.C.O. wounded	
	30		Carried on work on Dugouts & everts O.P's	

Vol 14

CONFIDENTIAL
No 3092 A
HIGHLAND
DIVISION

CONFIDENTIAL

War Diary

of

2/2ⁿᵈ Highland Field Co. R.E.(T.)

from 1ˢᵗ July 1916 to 31ˢᵗ July 1916.

WAR DIARY
INTELLIGENCE SUMMARY

Army Form C. 2118.

Place	Date	Hour	Summary of Events and Information	Remarks and references to Appendices
	1916		60th DIV.	
Mt ST ELOI	July 1		2 Sections 1/6 London Field Co attached to Sections to Thenalz for one breath. Remainder of Company unit attached to Headquarters at ST ELOI.	W.B.
	6		Carry on work in O.P. Section with Brigade Tramuel O.P.s	N.C.S.
	11		Hand over work to Tunnellers, workshops at Mt ST ELOI to 1/6 London Field Co 60th Div.	N.C.S.
	13		Company move back to TINQUE under orders for C.R.E. 5th Div.	N.C.S.
	14		Receive orders to be prepared to move on 1 hours notice & to change all extra kit in Salvage Dump Not	N.C.S.
	15		Dismounted Section move in motor lorries at 1am to DOULLENS. Mounted Section move to same place by road.	N.C.S.
	16		Receive Operation Orders at 3am to move at 7am to BOIS BERGUES	N.C.S.
	18		Stay at BOIS BERGUES. Inspect all equipment	N.C.S.
	19		Receive orders to be prepared to move on one hours notice. Receive Operation Order at 7pm to move immediately to MONTON VILLERS under C.R.E.	N.C.S.
	20		Arrive MONTON VILLERS 2am & receive Operation Order at 3am to move at 6am to RIBEMONT. Arrive there 5pm making a total travel from BOIS BERGUES of 36 miles	N.C.S.
	21		Receive orders to be prepared to move on one hours notice. Receive Operation orders from C.R.E. to move into area round BECOURT at 8pm.	N.C.S.

WAR DIARY
INTELLIGENCE SUMMARY

Army Form C. 2118.

Place	Date	Hour	Summary of Events and Information	Remarks and references to Appendices
BECOURT	1916 JULY 22		Receive orders to put a platoon in each of the 3 advanced dumps D4, X, D5. O.C. attends at G.S. in afternoon & receives orders to send 2 sections Sappers to dig more trenches in line BAZENTIN LE GRAND – BAZENTIN LE PETIT. 2 Sections erect huts for Bn Hd Qs at FRICOURT & repair old German Dugouts. 1 Sapper wounded	A03
	23		All 4 Sections go on to Reserve Line with infantry working parties. 1 N.C.O wounded.	A03
	24		Same section ordered from Reserve line to repair trenches in Reserve Line. 200 workers Party for entrenching at FRICOURT slightly reinforced. 1 sapper slightly wounded.	A03
	25		Owing to heavy German Barrage on valley up to BAZENTIN one section cannot get through to work & therefore arrange they go into billets in German Dugouts in BAZENTIN LE GRAND	A05
	26		Nos 1 & 2 Sections move up at 3am to dugouts at BAZENTIN LE GRAND. Site several H Q Emplacements in Reserve Line & also R.T. to rear, 1 Sapper wounded.	A05
	27		No working parties available for work. Get orders to detail Lt PILLIN & No 1 Section to proceed Barnett Hydraulic Pipes being laid on trench route to HIGH WOOD & follow into C & D to German Line. Cannot work on Nos 3 & 4 proposed carried up	A05
	28		Carry on as above to continue relief with No 1 & 2 Sections – work delayed by German artillery fire	A05

Army Form C. 2118.

WAR DIARY
or
INTELLIGENCE SUMMARY.
(Erase heading not required.)

Place	Date	Hour	Summary of Events and Information	Remarks and references to Appendices
FRICOURT	1916 July 29		Capt WARREN goes to BAZENTIN LE GRAND to take command of detachments of 1/2nd 2/3rd Corps Htrs. Large Htr. burst 10.30 p.m. Nose at 10.30 p.m. 40ft behind noted as about 20' across the top, 8' deep. Black fumes, pieces forward from end of Htr burst forward a/c shells killed by aeroplane bomb & 1 slightly wounded by aeroplane	LC1.
	30		2/Hr wounded slightly & sent by aeroplane. Received operation order for CRE first another section goes to BAZENTIN LE GRAND to reinforce other section Htrs 1/153rd Bty. attack reinforce army transits among through Square S11a, S9a1, S9a2, R8 at BAZENTIN probably augmented to make 3 strong points (2 Sections 1/2)(1 Section 3/11) + 2 Section S/2 24th in reserve.	NC1
	31		R.E. at BAZENTIN LE GRAND not called upon. Finish strong points. CRE goes round front line with Capt WARREN + arranges for working parties to dig hrs front line as agreed explained night before on right of HIGH WOOD about 160' in front of previous line. Working parties distributed turn up at correct time & performed whole of there very loudly having been to attack prisoners tryh.	NC1.

51st Divisional Engineers.

2/2nd HIGHLAND FIELD COMPANY R. E.

AUGUST 1 9 1 6 ::::

WAR DIARY
or
INTELLIGENCE SUMMARY.

Army Form C. 2118.

Place	Date	Hour	Summary of Events and Information	Remarks and references to Appendices
BECOURT	1916 AUG 1		No 1 & 4 Section relieved 4.30 am at BAZENTIN LE GRAND by 2 sections 1/1st Coy. No 2 Section with 200 working party start 33 entrances for dugouts in bank on road at X29.b.4.5. The entrances to be all connected up by gallery. 30' between each entrance. 1 Sapper wounded on this job. Entrance with new front line.	WS
	2		Capt WARREN hands over command of obliteration at BAZ. LE GRAND to Lt McCROME 1/1st & G. No 2 & 4 carrying on work on dugouts with 6 reliefs of 200 men ea + 20 carpenters making frames.	WS
	3		No 3 Section relieved by No 4 at 4.30 am. Carried on work on dugouts + new Font Lane.	WS
	4		No 3 Section relieves No 2 on dugouts. Carry on there and new Font Lane. No 2 Section gets working party 300 men for new Communication Trench between GEORGE ST + LEITH WALK already laid out by No 4 Section with double tapes 3'6" apart to give elbow guidance to Infantry.	WS
	5		Carried on with dugouts till 8 pm when did not work at night on them owing to scarcity of water for frames class carried on with new Font Lane + new Comn Trench.	WS
	6		No 4 Section return to BECOURT during morning. Receive O.O. from C.R.E. that company will move to new Bivouacs at 4 pm, but that in consulted RE, morning of 7th that 1 Section goes up to BAZENTIN to take over Capt Young Jack from the 1/1st Coy with instructions	WS

WAR DIARY or INTELLIGENCE SUMMARY.

Army Form C. 2118.

Place	Date	Hour	Summary of Events and Information	Remarks and references to Appendices
BECOURT	1916 Aug 6		to hand over to Field Co of 33rd Div. who would arrive relief in early hours of 7th.	WD
	7		No 1 Section arrives Becourt early having left Bazentin & company hours to Buires N of Dernancourt + is affiliated with 152nd Inf. Brig during move.	WD
	8		Transport moves at 4pm from Buires dusk 152nd Brig. Transport to CARDONETTE	WD
	9		Dismounted parade for entraining at 5pm at EDGE HILL (near Dernancourt) Owing to delay trains does not move till 3.30 a.m. Detrained at LONGPRE' march to SOREL Road. Lt GRANT returns to duty from leave.	WD
	12		SOREL Transport moves from CARDONETTE to PONT REMY 4 Road. Lt GRANT arrives at PONT REMY to entrain. Parade 3.30 a.m. entrained 5.30 a.m dismounted + march to STEEN BECQUE at 4 pm. March for STEEN BECQUE. Train moves at 8 am + arrives STEENBECQUE at 8am to BLARINGHEM.	WD
	13		Moved one Officer + 1 NCO to EBBLINGHEM to go by bus to forward area to take over from Field Co at present in line.	WD
	17		Remain at BLARINGHEM, Gas handling meeting instruction to 152nd Brigade with a view to going into line of trenches again.	WD
	18		Transport leaves off 4.30 am to proceed by road to ARMENTIERES. Dismounted entrain at EBBLINGHEM for STEENWERCK thence by road to ARMENTIERES.	WD

WAR DIARY or INTELLIGENCE SUMMARY

Army Form C. 2118.

Place	Date	Hour	Summary of Events and Information	Remarks and references to Appendices
ARMENTIERES	1916 Aug 19.		Receive reinforcement 2 officers 119 other Ranks.	
			Up and prepared work parties convert of concrete dugouts in Subsidiary Line & more preparation for demolition of bridge over River LYS in Divisional Area.	
	21		Get all arrangements made for 1 Sappers trade to each Coy for work in dugouts + 30 men carrying to each dugout.	
	22		Start 7 dugouts working carrying parties on left found by 153rd Bry &154 Bry on Right. Carrying parties do not turn up to time. No 1 Section working on Bridges & Artillery O.P.'s. Horses casualty of two Limbers maid lame.	
	24		Carry on works as above. Task up 30 tons stones every night to keep concrete plates going. Receive reinforcement 3 O.R., Lt RAE gets 3 weeks park leave (Hampshire)	
	26/27		Carry on as above + start strengthening with Pipe Young fork with a view to cutting enemy wire also with Bangalore Torpedoes. Enemy were in this locality 25 to 30" wide. LT A.C. Hill returns to duty from Base.	
	29		LT GRANT taken up duty at R.E. Headquarters as D.A.R.E.	
	31		Carry on works as above.	

Jn Broom Major R.E. (T.)
O.C. 2/2nd Highland Field Co. R.E.

CONFIDENTIAL.
No 21/A.
HIGHLAND
DIVISION.

VR/16

CONFIDENTIAL.

War Diary.

of

2/2ⁿᵈ Highland Field Co. R.E.(T.)

from 1st September 1916. to 29th September 1916.

WAR DIARY
or
INTELLIGENCE SUMMARY.
(Erase heading not required.)

Army Form C. 2118.

Instructions regarding War Diaries and Intelligence Summaries are contained in F. S. Regs., Part II. and the Staff Manual respectively. Title pages will be prepared in manuscript.

Place	Date	Hour	Summary of Events and Information	Remarks and references to Appendices
ARMENTIERES	1916 SEPT 1		Carry on work on concrete shelters. Experiment with Pipe Pushers & Bangalore Torpedoes for wire cutting	WS
	3		Give demonstration of wire cutting with above. Carry on work on concrete shelters	WS
	5		Carry on work on concrete shelters. Subsidiary line	WS
	13		Stop all work on concrete shelters. All sappers to be used as carrying parties on nights of 13/14, 14/15, 15/16, & 17/18 to make up 5 Bangalore torpedoes of 2" strove pipes for raids on night 15/16 & later. Also	WS
	14		our own wire 2 for 6 Leinsters 3 for 6 Gordons	WS
	15		2 torpedoes for 6 Leinsters but made Germen wire by them & blown by R.E. at 8.55pm clearing all wire - Raid very successful - 1 German + 27 killed in trenches 3 torpedoes for 6 Gordons took out and up to klin owing to myt General Heneral + an blown at varying times. Raiding parties did their job out.	WS
	18		Try to make torpedoes of 4.7.1" flat piping for 6 Gordons but the break away up	WS
	21		Made up 3 torpedoes 18', 18', 12". 2" water piping. These are placed on full sons	WS
	23		Torpedoes exploded in 2 cases the wire not cut but wiring have pushed through	WS

Army Form C. 2118.

WAR DIARY
or
INTELLIGENCE SUMMARY.
(Erase heading not required.)

Place	Date	Hour	Summary of Events and Information	Remarks and references to Appendices
ARMENTIERES	1916			
	Sept 23		Third torpedo shews all wires & raiding party got through, but owing to shell bursting	
	25		& burning ran of Hse, they have to return.	
	27		Handed over work to 8th Durham Field Co. & 2nd Field Co. R.E. & move to LA CRECHE.	
	29		Inspected mustered kits & equipment transport. Got remarks of Coy immaculate. Receive O.O. that Company will entrain at BAILLEUL for DOULLENS.	

W. Brown, Major R.E. (T.)
O.C. 2/2nd Highland Field Co. R.E.

Secret
VII/17

CONFIDENTIAL.
No 71
HIGHLAND DIVISION.

1st to 31st October 1916

CONFIDENTIAL.

WAR DIARY.

OF

2/2ND HIGHLAND FIELD Co. R.E.(T.)

from 1st October 1916.

CONFIDENTIAL Army Form C. 2118.
No 71 (A)
HIGHLAND DIVISION

WAR DIARY
or
INTELLIGENCE SUMMARY.
(Erase heading not required.)

Army Form C. 2118.

Instructions regarding War Diaries and Intelligence Summaries are contained in F.S. Regs., Part II. and the Staff Manual respectively. Title pages will be prepared in manuscript.

Place	Date 1916 Oct	Hour	Summary of Events and Information	Remarks and references to Appendices
GEZAINCOURT	1		Entrain at BAILLEUL for DOULLENS. March to GEZAINCOURT.	W.B.
	2		March with 152 Brigade to BOIS DE WARNIMONT. Billetted in little huts.	W.B.
	3		Reconnoitre HEBUTERNE Section which 152 Brigade take over till 19th Div. are up.	W.B.
	4		4 Section sent details move to Brigade at HEBUTERNE & work on main Up + Down C.T.	W.B.
	6		Headquarters, Transport at ROSSIGNOL FARM near COIGNEUX. Hand over billets & dumps at ROSSIGNOL FARM to 91st Fd Co. move to INVERNESS	W.B.
	7		field at COURCELLES. Call section out of HEBUTERNE. Look to COURCELLES. Start + make Recon HQ	W.B.
			Dumps in VERCINGETORIX.	
	9		Work on Improvement of HQ. Communication Trench JEAN BART. RE Dumps. Bridges	W.B.
			for field artillery to advance + Ambulances	
	12		Entrain work on above + dig new portion of JEAN BART + assembly trench. Recon Reinforced	5 O.R.
	14		Arrange to start work on 2 Bridges for Tanks. Recon road for that all	W.B.
	15		working parties cancelled.	W.B.
	16		Receive orders to be prepared to move at short notice.	W.B.
	16/17		Moved by bus for various homes.	W.B.

1577 Wt.W10791/1773 500,000 7/15 D.D. & L. A.D.S.S./Forms/C. 2118.

WAR DIARY
INTELLIGENCE SUMMARY

Army Form C. 2118.

Place	Date	Hour	Summary of Events and Information	Remarks and references to Appendices
MAILLY-MAILLET	1916 OCT 18		Receive orders to move to wood South of MAILLY-MAILLET. 3 Sections to be in shelters in wood. 1 Section in RE Dump MAILLY. Receive orders to get working party to dig trenches l'Ocelot	V.B.
	19		from MARLBOROUGH Trench to CLIVE ST + to lay reflector in the following night. Those to be assembly trenches	
	20		Explode this trench – result not very satisfactory owing to chalk surface. Rear assembly trench cancelled. Reference 3.D.R. received. Dig out the above assembly trench. All carpenters work in toolshed &c at RE Dump. Also work on 4th Avenue.	V.B.
	21		Work on assembly trench & complete, stores, + G.T's. Headquarters transferred over to FORCEVILLE	V.B.
	23		3 sections detailed for work under Brigade 1 under C.R.E. work as above. Operations postponed 24 hours.	V.B.
	24		LT BIRNIE reported by Listener as missing. Messenger sent to Listening Trench where he &	V.B.
	25.		action working in RE Dump but no one came if LT BIRNIE there. LT BIRNIE's body found buried under flying Traverse. Look worked connecting up dugouts in HESTON STREET. NCO's work on 4th & 2nd Avenues. Operations postponed 48 hrs.	V.B.
	26		LT BIRNIE buried in cemetery at MAILLY-MAILLET. Carry on work on 4th + 2nd Avenue. Operations postponed a further 48 hours.	V.B.
	27		Carry on as above	V.B.

Army Form C. 2118.

WAR DIARY
or
INTELLIGENCE SUMMARY.
(Erase heading not required.)

Instructions regarding War Diaries and Intelligence Summaries are contained in F. S. Regs., Part II. and the Staff Manual respectively. Title pages will be prepared in manuscript.

Place	Date	Hour	Summary of Events and Information	Remarks and references to Appendices
FORCEVILLE	1916 Oct 29		Work on 472 Avenue whitewing to bad weather required constant work	425 L/S
	31		Operation postponed to Nov 5.	
			[signed] Major R.E. (T.) O.C. 2/2nd Highland Field Co. R.E.	

CONFIDENTIAL.

War Diary.

of

2/2ⁿᵈ HIGHLAND FIELD Co. R.E.(T.)

from 1ˢᵗ Nov. 1916.

to 30ᵗʰ Nov. 1916.

Army Form C. 2118.

WAR DIARY
or
INTELLIGENCE SUMMARY
(Erase heading not required.)

Place	Date	Hour	Summary of Events and Information	Remarks and references to Appendices
FORCEVILLE	Nov 1916			
	1		Handed dugout wounded whilst taking up stones to WHITE CITY highway being filled under his [?].	JHb.
	3		Worked on 4th & 2nd Avenues which had fallen in badly with heavy rain. Enlarged enlarging starting dugouts. Made Gumboot store in Mailly & drying huts in Combes.	JHb.
	7		Worked on above & placed gas curtains in CTs.	JHb.
	9		Continued as above also enlarging dugout for Hdqs 6th Infantry. also huts at 6 Jonkers. Camp at FORCEVILLE.	JHb.
	10		Owing to exceptionally heavy rain 4th & 2nd Avenues left almost levelled to parts by falls in. Got working party 700 men to repair these from 152 Brig.	JHb. JHb.
	11		Got further working party 400 men to complete 4 & 2 Avenues. Got instructions that Field Coy Commanders are responsible that CTs are works for Z day & Y day notice that this is X day. 2 Drivers wounded & 3 horses killed by bomb from [?].	JHb.
	12		Got 100 working party on 4th Avenue & got instructions to complete 2 overland tracks to Tommy into Russo lengths.	JHb.
	13		Z day. Wait to receive for instructions. 152 & 153 Brigades attack at 5.45 am + capture BEAUMONT-HAMEL, GREEN LINE, + MUNICH TRENCH.	JHb.
	14		Receive orders at 10 am that all sections will proceed to dugouts CRIPPS CUT [?] for Offrs. & JCOs. [?].	JHb.

1577 Wt. W10791/1773 500,000 1/15 D.D. & L. A.D.S.S./Forms/C. 2118.

WAR DIARY or INTELLIGENCE SUMMARY

Army Form C. 2118.

Place	Date	Hour	Summary of Events and Information	Remarks and references to Appendices
FORCEVILLE	Nov 1916 14 (Cont)		& work under instructions B.G.C. 152 Inf Brig in consolidation.	
	15.		Hdqrs at WHITE CITY. During Night 12 noon receive instructions from Brigadier MAJOR BISSET stays with Brigade is Captured "C" to make 2 strong points Consolidate MUNICH TR. at right with 2 Sections R.E. & 1 platoon 8 R.S. & to replaced 8 R.S. + 2 Section R.E. & 1 Platoon R.S. & Strong Points are worked on for 11 hours continuously by one party & finished steep wiring. The MUNICH TR. party & 8 arrival find MUNICH TR. still held by Germans who start to bomb the working party as they come up LEAVE AV. A new trench is therefore dug about 150 x behind as an forming up & jumping off place for further operations. 2 Lt McFADYEN + 5 O.R. are wounded in BEAUMONT HAMEL. 2 Platoon detrenched 2 section R.E. dig (partially) line another Strong Point & BEAUMONT ALLEY + also partially wire the one dug in LEAVE AV. 4 O.R. wounded.	8 Rs. 8 Rs. 8 Rs.
	16		1 Lt WILSON 1 O.R. wounded. New Consolidation wiring of Strong Points. 2 in and new C.T. from LEAVE AV to Left of New MUNICH TR. Laid away to working party turning to SS in place of R.O. are unable to start it & improve ZERNE AV inclined. Last half MUNICH TR. is still in German hands & C.T. could not be taken further that NEW MUNICH TR. Receive instructions to move back to original billets after work. Receive reinforcement 18 O.R.	Memor 9/9 B.C. 2/7 High Ld Bn Red.I.Rn

WAR DIARY or INTELLIGENCE SUMMARY

Army Form C. 2118.

Place	Date	Hour	Summary of Events and Information	Remarks and references to Appendices
FORCEVILLE	Nov 1916 17.		Move out of trenches to huts MAILLY WOOD EAST & Holy at FORCEVILLE.	O.R.bs.
	18-19		1 Sec. deepened and extended Strong Point on LEAVE AVE. Later known as STEWART WORK. 1 Sec. along with 10P 8th Royal Scots commenced HARPER WORK on the North end of BEAUMONT HAMEL — Strong Point of Observation Type. O.R.s.	O.R.bs.
	19-20		1 Sec. with 30 Royal Scots carried on with HARPER WORK.	O.R.bs.
	20		HAMILTON WORK, another Strong point, was commenced by 1 Sec. with 30 Inf. at the South End of BEAUMONT HAMEL. No. 945 Pte. W. CALDER proceeded the Military Medal D.R.O. No. 647 x dated 20.11.16 Pte Roys P.O.W. 1 Sec. carried on with HAMILTON WORK. 75' C.T. completed.	O.R.bs.
	21		Trench and M.G. Emplacement made.	O.R.bs
	22		1 Sec. completed BURN WORK near entrained front line N. of BEAUMONT ROAD. Along with 50 Inf. This place made a C.T. deepened. 1 Sec. completed CAMPBELL WORK near entrained front line S. of BEAUMONT ROAD along with 50 Inf. Excavation & wiring completed. 1 Sec. & 50 Inf. completed HAMILTON WORK. Trench deepened and 60' additional C.T. dug towards BEAUMONT HAMEL.	

Known Capt. & field N O.B.E.D
for O.C. 2/1 Highland C.F.R.E.B

Army Form C. 2118.

WAR DIARY
or
INTELLIGENCE SUMMARY.
(Erase heading not required.)

Place	Date	Hour	Summary of Events and Information	Remarks and references to Appendices
FORCEVILLE	Nov 1916 22		No 3 Coy came from MAILLY WOOD to FORCEVILLE	
	23		Coy. entrained at FORCEVILLE	
BOUZIN-COURT	27		Coy. moved to BOUZINCOURT with 152nd Brigade	
OVILLERS POST	28		Coy. moved up to huts at OVILLERS POST the following day. Took over the three companys of COURCELETTE from the 4th CANADIAN Div. Sub nr. OVILLERS POST unmounted and bivy	yes yes yes yes
	29		but put on order. This noticed snow running	yes
	30		Reconnoitre AVELUY WOOD for transport and trench yes.	
				J. Kearns Capt. </br> ro o/c 1/1 High. Field Coy R.E.

CONFIDENTIAL.
No 71(A)
HIGHLAND DIVISION.

Vol 19

CONFIDENTIAL

WAR DIARY

OF

2/2ⁿᵈ HIGHLAND FIELD Co. R.E.(T).

from 1ˢᵗ December 1916. to 31ˢᵗ December 1916.

WAR DIARY
or
INTELLIGENCE SUMMARY

Army Form C. 2118.

Place	Date	Hour	Summary of Events and Information	Remarks and references to Appendices
OVILLERS POST	1916 DEC. 1		Commence manufacture of duckboard mats in AVELUY WOOD for Divisional Roads in forward area. Reconnoitre of front line by Capt DAVIS. H.Q. in OVA HILL. Coby in OVILLERS POST. 1 Officer & 50 O.R. Infantry attached for work.	
	2		Commence improvement of AVELUY WOOD Camp & bath-rugby.	
			Major BISSET OPES in Command. 10 O.R. reporting sick etc.	
	3		Dine in hutments. Bath supply & workshop and runnell 2 officers and 32 Coy in hutments.	
			66 O.R. Infantry attached for work and SAWMILL.	
			Constructed attacked line defences for work on sawmill. Commence erection of New huts.	
	4		supply to R.A.M.C. at East End of WOLSELEY HUTS.	
	5		Commence felling trees for saw in AVELUY WOOD. Commence making new sawmill. Emplacements for bases at PIONEER ROAD SIDING to HUTS. Phillips in front line. 1 officer reinforcement received. 11 Lt R.S.W. PATERSON.	
	6		Two trips 100 men of 152nd Brigade in rapid supply. For instruction of job. Propagateds in BOUZINCOURT.	
	7		Reinforcement of 9 O.R. received.	
	8		Recce trenches again to relieve 1/1st Highland F.C.	
	9		Unmoved oneh to 1/1st High field by Major Lyons with Phillips in WOLFE HUTS.	
			40 BOXCELS. Took over work of 1/1st High forces by Paterson. 2 men of 66 B.R. attacked by High Lines. Three ale made of 4 off and 100 O.R. (Officer Mostr)	
LA BOISELLE	9/10		Commence changing IRONSIDE AVENUE (OVILLERS-COURCELETTE TRENCH) with Potions Mattrs and roads. Parts of 200.	

Paterson O/C

Army Form C. 2118.

WAR DIARY
or
INTELLIGENCE SUMMARY
(Erase heading not required.)

Instructions regarding War Diaries and Intelligence Summaries are contained in F. S. Regs., Part II. and the Staff Manual respectively. Title Pages will be prepared in manuscript.

Place	Date	Hour	Summary of Events and Information	Remarks and references to Appendices
LA BOISELLE	1916 DEC. 10		Gunners go via 2nd Martin Batt. tunnel WOLFE HUTS. Reg't Party returned from France and brought ammunition to Brigade HQ at Albert. & III Corps School of Instruction. Experience continuing.	
	10/11		Carry went to IRONSIDE AVENUE, no stores. Brigade laying continued. Overland route with plywood mats. Unit lodging to TOURCELETTE tunnel, first this month – numbers 100 . 5 flrs.	
	11/12		Carry on with overland route and IRONSIDE AVENUE. Unit not finished with felt line. Tunnel bring day 8' inc. at 2' 6" at bottom and 5' 6" slope. flrs.	
	12		Review members. regt Bosieres. flrs.	
	12/13		Reserve reinforcement of flrs. flrs.	
			Battery overland route, ramps and BOZIERES. flrs. WEST MIRAUMONT (Gunshaft) ROAD. Look on IRONSIDE AVE. Difficult, many planners leaving carried to DYKE ROAD not tried.	
	13		Amplification greater - ALVE Hastings Ruts. at WOLFE HUTS. Brigade. pilot of ditto at gun post J. Side 1 mile IRONSIDE AVE. by day. flrs.	
	13/14		Carry on with overland Route, company to DYKE ROAD, and IRONSIDE AVENUE. D.D.A. MACKAY wounded. flrs.	
	14		Carry on with Route Two and IRONSIDE AVE. Old WARGREEN attached. Conference at Div HQ. flrs.	
	15		Carry on with Two Route Two. flrs.	
	16		Carry on with Two Route Two IRONSIDES AVENUE. 2/ Lieut Lovell's 5 Field no 73 Batt'n Heavy Gatling M.G.E. flrs.	
	16/17		Carry on with Overland Route Two and IRONSIDE AVE. Parties sunk to 33 Rgt. Inf. Batt. H.Q. 370 card flrs.	

[signature]

WAR DIARY
or
INTELLIGENCE SUMMARY
(Erase heading not required.)

Army Form C. 2118.

Place	Date	Hour	Summary of Events and Information	Remarks and references to Appendices
LA BOISELLE	1916 DEC			
	17/18		Manoeuvred Coy to Central Northwards along EAST MIRAUMONT ROAD from C Dump. 9/Ls.	
	18/19		Coy is/typed 150' Louing heavy head. 9/Ls.	
	19		Immense cel shelter for sheeny bations at CRICHTON'S POST 9/Ls.	
	19/20		Overlayed workes mainland out with 4'6" plates & wire furis to Bn/H.Q.	
			B Dump not to MANCHESTER SUMP 2500'. 9/Ls.	
			Shops this completed — Depour had with loose expeled, is transfel	
	20		[illegible] trans conded. (No pittel not flove frook), met shelter for Byl. WARREN attende conference in	
			Bnd H.Q.	
	30/11		Overland Route tapedfrom C Dump to A Dump. 300' includity 400' of IRONSIDE AVE. includity small, 300' mine lackly done. 9/Ls.	
	21		Happel own trike to 1/1 Highld Lt Cy of Tebe own trule workout trie from the attacked to 13 th Bgde for work. CAPT WARDEN attends conference 9/Ls.	
	21/22		91. Mqdo H.Q.	
			Dimlerh trench shelks employed shis Cy intrefriched by 1/c 14. F.C.	
	22		Receive 1 officer reinforcement vig. 2/Lt G.R. SCOTLAND.	
	22/23		3 trench shelter elected in front line, instructed of 4 howard head coming to 9/Ls.	
	23/24		5 trench shelter erected or front end of IRONSIDE AVE. 9/Ls.	
			Commence note at front end of IRONSIDE AVE. Carry on with IRONSIDE AVE 9/Ls.	
	24/25		3 trench shelter elected infront line. Carry on with IRONSIDE AVE 9/Ls.	
	25/26			

J.H.Brown Capt.

Army Form C. 2118.

WAR DIARY
or
INTELLIGENCE SUMMARY
(Erase heading not required.)

Instructions regarding War Diaries and Intelligence Summaries are contained in F. S. Regs., Part II. and the Staff Manual respectively. Title Pages will be prepared in manuscript.

Place	Date	Hour	Summary of Events and Information	Remarks and references to Appendices
LA BOISELLE	1916 DEC 26		CAPT. WARREN attacks captured at Bde H.Q. Pls.	
	26/27		No work done owing to continued snow showers by Rambury and Drouet at front line. Attached tool rolls & 150 2" Bydes. Pls.	
	27/28		154 Bg Cde relieved by 152 Bygde. Pls.	
	28/29		Coy moved to IRONSIDE AVE. 3 holes created in parapet but cover north IRONSIDE AVE. Pls.	
	29/30		Coy moved IRONSIDE AVE. to thatcherecks nupsholes & 1 in front line. Pls.	
	30/31		1 shelter erected in front line + 1 in M.G. position. Pls.	
	31/1		12" Firebay widened in front line (from No 15) 40 ft of knife boards put into IRONSIDE AVE. 200' aeroplane at thereby. Pls.	

[signature] *R.E. (T.)*

O.C. 2/2nd Highland Field Co. R.E.

CONFIDENTIAL
No 21(A)
HIGHLAND
DIVISION.

WD26

CONFIDENTIAL

WARY DIARY.

OF

404 2/2ND HIGHLAND FIELD Co. R.E.(T)

from 1st January 1917.
to 31st January 1917.

WAR DIARY or INTELLIGENCE SUMMARY

Army Form C. 2118.

CONFIDENTIAL
No 21(A)
HIGHLAND DIVISION

Place	Date	Hour	Summary of Events and Information	Remarks and references to Appendices
LA BOISELLE	1917 JAN 1		Receive orders to move to OVILLERS POST Laurnil on 2nd	
	2		Relieved in front line west by 1/1st Argyll. Move to Laurnil. Coy opp. fort from 2/4 and Coy. 1/1st Coy Groymith Sawmill. Resume work on AVELUY WOOD. 1/1st Coy mill., felling trees, and entraining timberwood; 2nd and 4th Coys. + Supplies wrote employed on this Sandentry fence by 9th Coy, Nissen huts for R.A.M.C. at OVILLERS HUTS Camp in vicinity of Martin Post. BOUZINCOURT. Repairs to Artillery road.	1/Ar. 1/Ar. 1/Ar.
	7		Receive D.O.O. No 126 for relief of Division by 2nd Division on 12/13th January. Company to march to PUCHVILLERS on 12th January in support for BUIGNY and to PUCHVILLERS on 13th January in support for 2/Lt P.D. DONALD Arr. reports joining 2/Lt P.D. DONALD Arr. Receive 1 Officer	1/Ar. 1/Ar.
	9		Offrs. mats. drive woodentting party, and construction & laundry, Party to Sawmill returns tothat unit.	1/Ar.
	10		2 Lt. G.J. ALLAN proceeds on motor lorry to Rail Head arr. with 21 Officers 1 Officer C.S.M 1/2 CSM 1/10 mu. Coast Angles For Bg	1/Ar.
	11		Annie to take over.	1/Ar.
PUCHVILLERS	12		March to PUCHVILLERS and arr. under orders of 153 Brigade. 2/Lt J.R.H.E. and 12 O.R. left at Sawmill to Survenill are.	1/Ar.
	13		Receive orders to move 1st Off & 80 O.R. to St Away Project School ST RIQUIER on 14	1/Ar.

J. Osborne Capt
R.E.O

WAR DIARY
or
INTELLIGENCE SUMMARY

Army Form C. 2118.

Place	Date 1917	Hour	Summary of Events and Information	Remarks and references to Appendices
GEZAINCOURT	Jan 14		1 Off. + 8 O.R. marched to GEZAINCOURT & thoroughly inspected billetting school at ST RIQUIER. Enfantry Offs. moved to GEZAINCOURT.	
CRAMONT	15		Company marches to CRAMONT.	
LE TITRE	16		Company marches to LE TITRE and funds (?) both wherever and stables near R.E. Dumps at LE TITRE and NOUVION.	
	17		Informed company drills &B.	
	19		No 2 Section breaks down huts at NOUVION. 2 Sections hutting at LE TITRE.	
	20		Continues hutting at LE TITRE.	
	22		Continues hutting at LE TITRE Lys.	
	23/31		Platoon firing in physical exercises, musketry drill with arms, bayonet and clothing(?), musketry instruction & fire practice. Grown kinder dust(?) + driving.	

M. Stewart, Major R.E. (T.)
O.C. 2/1st Highland Field Co. R.E.

Vol 21.

CONFIDENTIAL

War Diary

of

404TH (HIGHLAND) FIELD Co. R.E. (T)

from 1st February 1917.

to 28th February 1917.

Army Form C. 2118.

INTELLIGENCE SUMMARY

(Erase heading not required.)

Place	Date	Hour	Summary of Events and Information	Remarks and references to Appendices
LE TRE	1917 Feb 1		Receive notice that some of Company will return to 404 K (Highland) Field Co R.E.	VS
	3		Continued training	
	4		Major BISSET returning from 1st Corps School to resume command. Continued training. Capt WARREN receives instructions to proceed to PREYS & take over command of H.Q. 400 (H) Fd Co R.E. during next leave of Major Anson. Recce O.O. to move to L'ABBAYE D'AMONT Farm on 5th inst with 152nd Inf Brigade group.	VS VS VS
	5		Move to L'Abbaye d'Amont Farm. Transport has difficulty on hills owing to ice.	VS
	6		Move to ROUGEFAY.	VS
	7		Move to HERICOURT.	VS
	8		Move to OSTREVILLE	VS
	9		Move to CAUCOURT	VS
	10		Stay at CAUCOURT	VS
	11		Move under orders from C.R.E. to MARDEUIL.	
	12		Start work in Adv. Div. Hdq. estn. now from 401st Co. 2 stations in continuous reliefs. Inform Billets. Got 100 sappers has attacks	VS
	13		MAJOR BISSET goes to course at LE PARCQ. Lt GRANT assumes command. Sect 2 goes to line to trenches recce near Batt. C.O. at the line.	VS
	14		No 3 section starts work improving COLLECTEUR TRENCH	VS

WAR DIARY or INTELLIGENCE SUMMARY

Army Form C. 2118.

(Erase heading not required.)

Place	Date	Hour	Summary of Events and Information	Remarks and references to Appendices
MARCOEUIL	FEB 1917 15		No 3 Section working on COLLECTEUR. 4 Tramway on Ram=Bay No 2 Station " " " " B.G. Ammunition " No 1 " " " Adv. Dn Rely No 4 " " " do	
	16		Carry on as above. CAPT. BLAIR attached for 10 days Instruction	105.
	17		Work as above. 10 Carpenters attached for work	105.
	18		Commence work on OLD FANTOME Trench.	105.
	19		Carry on as above	105.
	20		No 3 Section relieves No 2. No 1 relieves No 3. LT WALLACE & 10 men detailed for work on T.M. emplacements under D.T.M.O.	105.
	21		Carry on as above. Sgt 3 R.A.C. Wagons attacked.	105.
	24		Work as above. LT TELFORD makes reconnaissance of dugout accomodation to Left Sub Sector. 1 Off. 50 Sappers	105.
	25		Did debs. 1 Off. 50 Sappers take report for duty. Experiment with mobile charges.	105.
	26		Carry on as above.	105.
	27		Carry on as above	105.
	28		No 2 Section relieves No 1 on GRAND COLLECTEUR & No 3 relieves No 4 on R.G. FANTOME AVS.	105.

Major R.E. (T.)
O.C. 404 (Highland) Field Co. R.E.

Vol 22

CONFIDENTIAL.

WAR DIARY

of

404TH (HIGHLAND) FIELD Co. R.E.(T.)

from 1st March 1917. to 31st March 1917.

Army Form C. 2118.

WAR DIARY
or
INTELLIGENCE SUMMARY.
(Erase heading not required.)

Instructions regarding War Diaries and Intelligence Summaries are contained in F. S. Regs., Part II. and the Staff Manual respectively. Title pages will be prepared in manuscript.

Place	Date	Hour	Summary of Events and Information	Remarks and references to Appendices
MARCEUIL	MARCH 1917 1.		Worked on A training Purposes A.G. FANTOME. COLLECTEUR, & Pelo Bro Holy, & Section living in ABRI CENTRAL LT WALLACE II Sappers working on T.M. emplacements	
	9		Carried on as above - Also work finished & extended to Garrison to maintain started on BIDOT post brancard from COLLECTEUR. Reamoured name not b top OA pill spread with a bus to pop a water supply.	
	12		Carried on as above. I destin goes to live at ABRI MOUTON. This makes 2 Section's Storekeepers	
	15		Cinema as above. A.G. badly damaged by retaliation to 2" trench mortar, started work for	
	16		Co cross country track from MAROEUIL to ROCLINCOURT.	
	19		started forming Pelu Bri Dumps at ROCLINCOURT & Brig Dumps at LES SABLIER. started filling shell holes to C.T's being worked on, marked along tramway ABRI MOUTON & for use as an OUTPOST.	
	22		Conference with C.R.E. Company Commander. In case of possible relieved of Germans offs all C.T's Work for 2 days to go on to deliver all C.T's. Reserve reinforcement 10 attacks on to 10 to Cross country track finished	
	23		Clear FANTOME, BLANCHARD & BIDOT C.T's	
	24		Carry on as above work on Pelu Bro Holy practically finished.	

WAR DIARY

INTELLIGENCE SUMMARY

Place	Date	Hour	Summary of Events and Information	Remarks and references to Appendices
MARŒUIL	1917 MARCH 25		No. 2 Section goes up to last A3R1 CENTRAL. Remainder 3 Sections to trenches, work on entrances to 2 Batt H^qrs, 1 Brig H^q, Fantôme Av, Collecteur, Bidot, AVG & latrine from rear to trench shelters.	
	26		Carried on as above — Reinforcement 1 O R.	
	27		5th Gordon Sappers helping majors Battalion got 75 1/7 ArGH trenches.	
	28		Handover 50 1/8 ArGH to 40th C^o as Sappers leave.	
	29		Lt Col WEEKS dropped down line and MAJOR J G FLEMING DSO appointed acting OC.	
	30		Stop all A tunnel works not trench revetments instead. No 2 makes gun trench & starts on enlarging dugouts in COLLECTEUR.	

Major R.E. (T.)
O.C. 1/404th (Highland) Field Co. R.E.

CONFIDENTIAL

War Diary

of

404th (Highland) Field Coy R.E.

from 1st to 30th April 1917.

Army Form C. 2118.

WAR DIARY
or
INTELLIGENCE SUMMARY.
(Erase heading not required.)

Instructions regarding War Diaries and Intelligence Summaries are contained in F. S. Regs., Part II. and the Staff Manual respectively. Title pages will be prepared in manuscript.

Place	Date	Hour	Summary of Events and Information	Remarks and references to Appendices
MAROEUIL	APRIL 1917			
	1		Carry on work on French off G.A. to tunnel heads & enlarging dug outs.	F.B
	3		Have conference with C.R.E. Final details arranged for X,Y,Z dugouts.	W.B.
	4		Have conference with 404 & 6 Officers & explain all details.	W.B.
	6		Carry on enlarging dugouts - forming Bn & Bde Adv Dumps etc.	W.B.
	8		Y day. at 6pm No 2 Section under LT RAE assemble in tunnel L27 ready to dig CT across No Man's Land. Interview possible in 2 days. No 1, 3, 4 sections Sappers & infantry assemble in shelters in HIGH ST ECURIE.	W.B.
	9		Z day. LT RAE reports about 12 noon that CT to WITTLESBACHER WEG completed to Craonchies. Receive instructions to reconnoitre & make Strong Point near COMMANDANTS HOUSE at 3 pm. 3 Sections RE Sappers take carry up stores from ROCLINCOURT to make Strong Point at B13 a 9.2. Light very quick, no enemy shelling, no casualties. Walked forward to BROWN LINE but failed to find any front Infantry, but G'nners of 153 Brigade who informed me that Germans still hold trenchyard in front.	F.B
	11		Company relieved by 2nd Div R.E. Go back to MAROEUIL. Receive instructions to move to ST NICHOLAS on 12 & to work under XVII Corps on BAILLEUL Road.	W.B.

WAR DIARY
or
INTELLIGENCE SUMMARY.

(Erase heading not required.)

Army Form C. 2118.

Place	Date	Hour	Summary of Events and Information	Remarks and references to Appendices
ST NICHOLAS (ARRAS)	APRIL 1917 12		Storm link route to ST NICHOLAS.	v.s.
	13		Start work on BAILLEUL Road. Work greatly hampered by traffic, & guns & wagons getting stuck in mud. Impossible to get material up owing to blocks. Corps refuse to stop traffic at all during day.	v.s.
	14		Weather very bad & traffic still very heavy on Road.	v.s.
	18		Continue work. Road now improving & traffic not so heavy.	v.s.
	19		Lay Decauville track to enable heavy Lorries to get Ammunition past the work place on road. Get 2 Companies Northumberland Fusiliers Pioneers	v.s.
	22		Road metal very scarce. Cut up tracks from ST NICHOLAS pending arrival of metal.	v.s.
	25		Carry on as about.	v.s.
	26		18th N.F. taken off Road & get 2 Companies 9th Seaforth Highlanders (Pioneers)	v.s.
	27		Hand over BAILLEUL Rd to XIII Corps & start work on ST LAURENT BLANGY Rd.	v.s.
	30		Carry on as above.	v.s.

Vol 24

CONFIDENTIAL

WAR DIARY

of

404TH (HIGHLAND) FIELD COY R.E. (T)

from 1ST to 31ST MAY 1917.

Army Form C. 2118.

WAR DIARY
or
INTELLIGENCE SUMMARY.
(Erase heading not required.)

Instructions regarding War Diaries and Intelligence Summaries are contained in F. S. Regs., Part II. and the Staff Manual respectively. Title pages will be prepared in manuscript.

Place	Date	Hour	Summary of Events and Information	Remarks and references to Appendices
ST NICHOLAS (ARRAS)	1917 MAY 1		Enlarge work on ST LAURENT BLANGY Rd. with 1 Batt 1/8 Royal Scots.	WD.
	3		Clear road through FAMPOUX for motor traffic.	WD.
	5		Clear high road through FAMPOUX. Receive orders for C.R.E. to be prepared for infantry relief.	WD
	6		Hand over work to 400th Field Co. & proceed to BAILLEUL AUX CORNAILLES.	WD.
	7/11		Train & overhaul at BAILLEUL AUX CORNAILLES.	WD.
	12		Move to ARRAS.	WD.
	13		Move to Railway Embankment on BLANGY-FAMPOUX Road. #1 Section reports to 152 Bgy for consolidation in event of attack proving successful. 1 Section report 152 M.G. Co. for M.G. emplacements. 2 Section & 155 Infantry dig C.T. COLON forward to CORONA.	WD.
	14		This section makes 2 Strong Points at W end of ROEUX. 1 Section makes M.G. emplacement WD in new front line captured on 13th inst.	WD
	15		Heavy enemy shelling of trenches all day. Sections down in evening - 3 Sections go out at 11.p.m. to make strong points at E end of ROEUX. Ohng to darkness	WD.

Army Form C. 2118.

WAR DIARY
or
INTELLIGENCE SUMMARY.

(Erase heading not required.)

Instructions regarding War Diaries and Intelligence Summaries are contained in F. S. Regs., Part II. and the Staff Manual respectively. Title pages will be prepared in manuscript.

Place	Date	Hour	Summary of Events and Information	Remarks and references to Appendices
ARRAS	1917 MAY 15		Platn attack did not go & front line before daylight. Took therefore unfavorable. Enemy counter attack at dawn. 2 drivers wounded taking position from Railway Embankment.	VA
	16		Counter attack by 152 Brig delays getting out trench till 9 p.m. Tried to take platn & check, work again unfavorable. Were later up to land in E. end of ROEUX dumped in CORONA.	VA
	17		Were in E. end of ROEUX to hand in a Rum SCARPE trench along front at E. end of village. Many Germans seen hurrying about – apparently relief.	VA
	18		2 lachins Gun were right to river bank & strong point commenced on river bank. Sappers fired on from Strong Point. Had last night – 3 wounded. German Prisoner taken near river bank.	US
	20		Strong Point on Rive Bank completed & trench round E. of ROEUX strengthened.	VA
	22		Rive Bank S. of ROEUX wired.	VA
	24		CT round N. side of ROEUX Wood commenced leading from CUSP to CEMETERY at ROEUX.	VA
	26		Carry in as above.	US
	27.		Maus O.C. 63rd FIELD Co RE 9th DN round work a view to handing over.	US

Army Form C. 2118.

WAR DIARY
or
INTELLIGENCE SUMMARY.
(Erase heading not required.)

Instructions regarding War Diaries and Intelligence Summaries are contained in F. S. Regs., Part II. and the Staff Manual respectively. Title pages will be prepared in manuscript.

Place	Date	Hour	Summary of Events and Information	Remarks and references to Appendices
ARRAS	1917. MAY 28		Receive instructions to demolish apparent German bridge on R SCARPE S.J ROEUX, then turns out to be tree blown down with driftwood piled up against it. Then plan up work interfered with by German Patrols from South Bank.	A.8
	29		Continue C.T. make supply at ROEUX, water Supply completed.	A.8
	30		Handed over to 63rd L.T.C. to move by tram to AVERDOINGT	A.8
	31		Clean up transport wagons etc.	A.8

[signature]
Major R.E. (T.)
O.C. 404 Highland Field Co. R.E.

— CONFIDENTIAL —

WAR DIARY

OF

404ᵀᴴ (HIGHLAND) FIELD Cᴼʸ R.E.

FROM 1ˢᵀ TO 30ᵀᴴ JUNE 1917.

Army Form C. 2118.

WAR DIARY
or
INTELLIGENCE SUMMARY.
(Erase heading not required.)

Place	Date	Hour	Summary of Events and Information	Remarks and references to Appendices
AVERDOINGT	1917 JUNE 1/3		Clean up & generally overhaul from to CONTEVILLE with 152nd Inf Brig Group.	
CONTEVILLE	4		Move to RECLINGHEM with 152nd Inf. Brigade Group.	
"	6		Cleaning equipment etc. Section Drill	
"	7		Kit Inspection. Section Drill etc.	
"	8		Move to LONGUENESSE	
LONGUENESSE	9		Move to OUEST MONT	
OUEST MONT	10		Training. Section Navy Squad Drill, Grouping & Loosing res	
"	11		Do.	
"	12		Do. Pack Horse competition at EPERLECQUES and election	
"	13		Do. Horse show Do.	
"	14		Given to Inf. in Brigade Do.	
"	15		Entrain at WATTEN for CASSEL (see sketch of Belgium 28 m. = 25,000) to A.29.C. Central. Transport move independently to HERZEELE.	

Army Form C. 2118.

WAR DIARY
or
INTELLIGENCE SUMMARY.
(Erase heading not required.)

Instructions regarding War Diaries and Intelligence Summaries are contained in F. S. Regs., Part II. and the Staff Manual respectively. Title pages will be prepared in manuscript.

Place	Date	Hour	Summary of Events and Information	Remarks and references to Appendices
	June 1917			
A.29.C Chaklat	16		Daylight arrived. Cleaning up & making camp.	
"	17		Two sections moved up to Dep. Ore in Canal Bank in C25 D & H	
"	18		Forward station commenced work on construction of Villies	
"	19		1 section moved forward from Dar Head Qrs. to Canal Bank	
"	20			
"	21			
"	22			
"	23		Work continued on construction of shelters in Canal Bank, work	
"	24		has been hampered daily to a certain extent by enemy	
"	25		shelling which at times was very heavy, the dump of R.E.	
"	26		material at Railway College has to be moved to Essex	
"	27		Farm on account of enemy fire.	
"	28			
"	29			
"	30			

O.C. 421 (64th) Fd Coy R.E.

CONFIDENTIAL
No. 31(A)
HIGHLAND
DIVISION.

Vol 26

CONFIDENTIAL

WAR DIARY

OF

404TH (HIGHLAND) FIELD COY R.E. (T)

FROM 1ST TO 31ST JULY 1917.

WAR DIARY
or
INTELLIGENCE SUMMARY.
(Erase heading not required.)

Army Form C. 2118.

REF MAP BELGIUM. SHEET 28 NW 1/80000.

Place	Date	Hour	Summary of Events and Information	Remarks and references to Appendices
	JULY 1914			
A.29.C Central	1		Work was continued on Construction of Shelters in Canal Bank.	Reinforcements = 4 O.R's. Casualties = 2 O.R. wounded. JR
	2		ditto	Casualties = 1 O.R. wounded JR
	3			
	4		Work was continued on Construction of Shelters in Canal Bank.	
	5		During this period work was considerably hampered at times by enemy shelling	
	6			
	7			
	8		ditto	Reinforcements = 1 O + 2 O.R. JR
	9		Work continued on Shelters	JR
	10		ditto	JR
	11		ditto	JR
A.27.3.4	12		Rear Hdqrs & Transport moved to A.27.b.3.4. Work continued on Construction of Shelters in Canal Bank	JR
	13		ditto	Adv. Hdqrs JR
			and 3 Sections moved from Canal Bank to Bivouacs in field B.27.d.3.9	JR
	14		Work continued on Shelters in Canal Bank	Casualties = 1 O.R. wounded JR
	15		ditto	JR

WAR DIARY or INTELLIGENCE SUMMARY

Army Form C. 2118.

Place	Date	Hour	Summary of Events and Information	Remarks and references to Appendices
A27b34 REF MAP BELGIUM SHEET 28 NW 1/20,000	July 1917 16		Work was continued on Construction of Shelters in Canal Bank Reinforcements. Casualties - 1 O.R. wounded 6 O.R.s	
	17		ditto Casualties - 3 O.R.s wounded	
	18		ditto Casualties - 1 O.R. wounded	
	19		ditto	
	20		ditto	
	21		ditto Casualties - 1 O.R. wounded	
	22		Work was continued on Shelters in Canal Bank. 1 Section on AID POST at C.20.d.2.7. before + entrances, and also at work in dugout near FOCH FARM	
	23		ditto Casualties - 1 O.R. wounded	
	24		ditto Reinforcements - 3 O.R.s	
	25		Work was continued on Shelters in CANAL BANK, also	
	26		on AID POST and FOCH FARM Dugout.	
	27			
	28		ditto ditto 1 Section working with 4th T.R.E. on Shelters	
	29		ditto. 4 " Section moved up to ADV. HD.QRS.	
	30		Work finished on Shelters & Dugouts today.	

WAR DIARY
or
INTELLIGENCE SUMMARY.

Army Form C. 2118.

Place	Date	Hour	Summary of Events and Information	Remarks and references to Appendices
A.24.b.3.4.	July 31		Company employed on making road from KRUPPS FARM to SCHULERS EST. Passable for guns.	

CONFIDENTIAL

WAR DIARY

OF

404TH (HIGHLAND) FIELD COY R.E. (T)

FROM 1ST TO 31ST AUGUST 1917.

WAR DIARY or INTELLIGENCE SUMMARY

Army Form C. 2118.

Place	Date	Hour	Summary of Events and Information	Remarks and references to Appendices
A.27.b.34. Ref Map BELGIUM SHEET 28 N.W. 1/20000	AUGUST 1		2 Sections R.E. & 50 Sappers Make north on PILCKEM ROAD between KRUPPS FARM and 5 CHEMINS ESTAMINET getting road clear for barrage of guns.	JX
	2		2 Sections R.E. & 70 Sappers Make repairing road between BELOW FARM and GOURNIER FARM, and also from KEMPTON PARK to BOURNIER ROAD. Enemy shelling hampered work on this road. Casualties - 2 O.R's killed. 2 O.R's wounded.	JX
	3		1 Section R.E. & 50 Sappers Make north on PILCKEM ROAD as stated above. 3 Sections R.E. & 70 Sappers Make on GOURNIER ROAD. Enemy shelling again interfered with work on this road.	JX JX
	4		ditto Casualties - 8 O.R's wounded.	JX JX
	5		ditto Casualties - 1 OFF. wounded.	JX
	6		Work continued on PILCKEM ROAD and GOURNIER ROAD as stated above.	JX
	7		Company started work under XVIII CORPS repairing PILCKEM ROAD from junction with HUDDLESTON ROAD forward. Casualties - 2 O.R's wounded.	JX
	8		Work continued on PILCKEM ROAD north under CORPS.	JX
	9		ditto	JX
	10		ditto Casualties - 10 O.R. wounded.	JX
	11 12 13		Work continued on PILCKEM ROAD work under XVIII CORPS	JX

WAR DIARY or INTELLIGENCE SUMMARY

Army Form C. 2118.

Place	Date	Hour	Summary of Events and Information	Remarks and references to Appendices
A27B34	August 14		Started work on BOUNDARY ROAD. Double road with platting forward.	JK
	15		ditto	JK
	16		Started work on duckboard track from ADMIRALS ROAD at C14B72 (Sheet 28 N.W.) forward.	Casualties – 1 OR killed 1 OR died of wounds. 2 OR wounded. Reinforcements 1 OR. JK
	17 18 19 20 21 22		Work was carried on duckboard track. Single track was laid to road junction at C9c96.3.	JK Reinforcement = 2 ORs. Transfers – 1 OFR. 400th RE (H/9M) 1 OFR. to 401st RE (H/9M) JK
	23 24 25 26		Double of duckboard track commenced. Double duckboard track completed to Road Junction at C9c95.3.	JK
	27		Work was extended on BOUNDARY ROAD from ALGERIAN COT. forward. Double road with platting.	JK
	28		ditto	Attached Infantry – 4 OFF. 8/100 JK
	29		ditto	Royal Algerian Inhales 152nd Brigade Reinforcements – 2 ORs. JK

Army Form C. 2118.

WAR DIARY
or
INTELLIGENCE SUMMARY

(Erase heading not required.)

Place	Date	Hour	Summary of Events and Information	Remarks and references to Appendices
A27 b 34	AUGUST 30		Started work on Bathhouse, Drying Sheds & Bridge on CANAL BANK, and work in MURAT and SIEBE CAMPS including Rifle Ranges. ditto	
	31		ditto	

for Capt. & Adjut. C.
1st (Highland) R.E.

To be cont.

CONFIDENTIAL

WAR DIARY

OF

404ᵀᴴ HIGHLAND FIELD Cᵒʸ R.E.

FROM 1ˢᵀ TO 30ᵀᴴ SEPTEMBER 1917.

Army Form C. 2118.

WAR DIARY
or
INTELLIGENCE SUMMARY.
(Erase heading not required.)

Instructions regarding War Diaries and Intelligence Summaries are contained in F. S. Regs., Part II. and the Staff Manual respectively. Title pages will be prepared in manuscript.

Place	Date	Hour	Summary of Events and Information	Remarks and references to Appendices
A27 B 34	SEPT.			
	1		Carried on with work on Bathurst & Greenwich Pks on CANAL BANK East. Improvements in MURAT & SIEGE CAMPS including Rifle Range. Both camps for bathing in Greenwich Station at MINTY POST.	
	2		Carried on with works as above.	
A21 a 64	3		ditto. Reinforcement - 1 O.R.	
	4		Carried on with work as above. Engine shed charged	
	5		Shell fire on CANAL BANK. Started Coys Kitchen at NUISANCE house. Work as above. Started new Engine Shed on CANAL BANK	
	6		Improvement in MURAT CAMP completed. Carried on work as above. Steam Kitchen at MINTY POST C10c15 (ST JULIEN 28 N.W.) Coys Kitchen C10c9.55. Brackwerk entered knife from C10c0.58 to HURST PARK any from C9d9.5c to NUISANCE C.O.T.	
	7		Carried on work as above	
	8		ditto. Casualties - 2 O.R's wounded. 2 horses killed	
	9		Brickwerk tracks completed. Coys Kitchen completed. Other work	
			Carried on as above	

Army Form C. 2118.

WAR DIARY
or
INTELLIGENCE SUMMARY.
(Erase heading not required.)

Instructions regarding War Diaries and Intelligence Summaries are contained in F. S. Regs., Part II. and the Staff Manual respectively. Title pages will be prepared in manuscript.

Place	Date	Hour	Summary of Events and Information	Remarks and references to Appendices
	SEPT			
A21a64	10		Started work on duckwalk track from SCHEMIDS EST. to CANS TRENCH at C.27.d.2 (St Julien 28NW2). Working on Dressing Station at night	
			Rest. Improvements at SIEGE CAMP, and Sft Sapper Sfts	
	11		Range at SIEGE CAMP completed	R
			ditto Reinforcements 2 OR	
	17		Carried on as above Reinforcements 1 OR Casualties 10 R wounded	108
	20		2 day. Company moves hut section burned at to STEENBEEK to repair Duck bridge with pepper moles. Reinforcements 2 OR	115
	21		No 3 Section home up to Mon BULGARE to clean company dugouts for use	115
			as Bug Hdqs with others moles	
	22		No 2 Section moves up to BULOW FarG to clean up our dugouts for use	123
			as Bn Hd Qrs Hdq No 1 section carry on with Dressing Station	
	23		Took Officers of 67 Co RS around work to hand over 10 R wounded 7 OR Reinforcements	125
	24		Section return to MORAT CAMP. Relieved by 67 Co RS. Took back to Siege	A
			CAMP.	
	27		Company at SIEGE CAMP 5 Horses killed 8 wounded by enemy air raid	

A6915 Wt. W11422/M1160 350,000 12/16 D.D.&L. Forms/C/2118/14.

WAR DIARY
or
INTELLIGENCE SUMMARY.

(Erase heading not required.)

Army Form C. 2118.

Place	Date	Hour	Summary of Events and Information	Remarks and references to Appendices
	1917 Sept 10		Move from Siege Camp to new area at PROVEN for BAPAUME WEST	A/1
			J. Bryant. Major R.E. (T.) O.C. 404 Highland Field Co. R.E.	

CONFIDENTIAL

WAR DIARY

OF

404TH (HIGHLAND) FIELD Coy. R.E.

FROM 1ST TO 31ST OCTOBER 1917.

WAR DIARY
or
INTELLIGENCE SUMMARY.
(Erase heading not required.)

Army Form C. 2118.

Place	Date	Hour	Summary of Events and Information	Remarks and references to Appendices
ACHIET LE PETIT	1917 October 1		Arrive BAPAUME & march to ACHIET LE PETIT.	
	2		C/o my work both with 7th Co. R.E. next arrive & taking over.	
	3		No 3 Section shifts huts move to BOISLEUX to complete D.H.Q.	
	4		do do do to 5 Cavalry Shelter Camp near BOIRY BECQUERELLE these are	
	5		Reinforcements — 1 O.R.	
			Remainder of Coy and transport moved to BOIRY BECQUERELLE. T.I.c.73	
T.I.c.7.3	6		(Sheet 51B France) No 1 & 2 Section L Sappers made detailed on work on new area and hut-up	
	7		Carried on work as above	
	8			
	9			
	10			
	11			
	12		Reinforcements — 2 O.R.	

WAR DIARY
or
INTELLIGENCE SUMMARY.
(Erase heading not required.)

Army Form C. 2118.

Place	Date	Hour	Summary of Events and Information	Remarks and references to Appendices
T.L.C.7.3.	OCTOBER 1917 13		Carried on work as before. Attacked 2 Rifle Ranges in Rear Areas.	A
	14			
	15			
	16			
	17			
	18		Carried on work as above.	A
	19			A
	20			
	21			
	22		Reinforcements – 4 O.R.	
	23			
	24			
	25			
	26		Carried on work as above.	A
	27			
	28			

WAR DIARY
or
INTELLIGENCE SUMMARY.

(Erase heading not required.)

Army Form C. 2118.

Place	Date	Hour	Summary of Events and Information	Remarks and references to Appendices
15.7.c.	OCTOBER 1917 29		Carried on work - Sea areas, Cafes & Rifle Ranges	J.B.
	30		Rifle chutes returned to their ings. No 1.2.3 Sections	
			Moved to BEAULANCOURT. No 2&4 Sections to billets provided	J.B.
			to MONT EN ESCOURT.	
	31		Arranges for Orders in New Area	J.B.

CONFIDENTIAL

WAR DIARY

OF

404th (HIGHLAND) FIELD Coy R.E.

FROM 1st TO 30th NOVEMBER 1917.

WAR DIARY or INTELLIGENCE SUMMARY

Army Form C. 2118.

(Erase heading not required.)

Place	Date	Hour	Summary of Events and Information	Remarks and references to Appendices
MONTENESCOURT (Ref. LENS 11)	Nov 1917 1		2 Sections working on improvements to Billets & both horse & personnel lines	
			1 Section with No 1 Coy RE 1 Section with No 2 Coy RE improving Billets & accommodation in HAVRINCOURT WOOD (France 57.)	
	6		2 Sections working in HAVRINCOURT WOOD. 1 Section laying a water supply for bathhouse	
			Coy HQ near IZEL-LES-HAMEAU (LENS 11) 1 Section repairing Bathhouse	
	9		ditto	
	10		ditto	
	15		Carpenters – 10 R. unrelated Reinforcements 1 O.R.	
	16		2 Sections working HAVRINCOURT WOOD. Water supplies finished	
			Transport moved by night from MONTENESCOURT to COURCELLES LES COMTE (AULNY) 78	
	17		2 Sections & HQrs entrained at BEAUMETZ LES LOGES for BAPAUME, marched from the	
			to ROCQUIGNY. (LENS 11) Transport moved by night from COURCELLES LE COMTE to BAPAUME	
NEUVILLE BOURJONVAL (Ref. France 57c)	18		2 Sections, HQrs & Transport moved from ROCQUIGNY to NEUVILLE BOURJONVAL (Ref France 57c) where other 2 Sections joined Company	
	20		4 Sections moved at 3 a.m. to Billets in HAVRINCOURT WOOD (Ref France 57c)	
			1 Section repaired bridge over trench in wood for passage of artillery	
	21		4 Sections & 150 Sappers started work on road through Wood (Ref France 57c)	

WAR DIARY
or
INTELLIGENCE SUMMARY.
(Erase heading not required.)

Army Form C. 2118.

Place	Date	Hour	Summary of Events and Information	Remarks and references to Appendices
NEUVILLE- BOURJONVAL (Ref France 57c)	Nov 1917 22		4 Sections & Section Transport moved from HAVRINCOURT WOOD to about K24c5.2 (Ref France 57cNE) 1 Section reform a bridge & make a diversion in road in FESQUIERES. 3 Sections and Sappers Makes slow progress through FESQUIERES	JR
	24		4 Sections & Transport & Sappers Makes move back to billets in HAVRINCOURT WOOD. Sappers Makes up this move.	JR JR
	25		4 Sections & Transport moved from wood to front about K15.a.2.5 (Ref France 57cNE)	JR
	26		4 Sections worked under I Corps on road about K15.a along road & round	JR
	27		Repair of road and laying a double length from 45b4 (Ref France 57c NE by transport waggons	JR
	30		Carried on work as above. Work hindered by enemy shelling. Casualties (O.R.) killed	JR

1/12/17

[signatures]

CONFIDENTIAL

WAR DIARY

OF

404th HIGHLAND FIELD COMPANY R.E.

DECEMBER 1914.

Army Form C. 2118.

WAR DIARY
or
INTELLIGENCE SUMMARY.
(Erase heading not required.)

Place	Date	Hour	Summary of Events and Information	Remarks and references to Appendices
Rear H.Qs	1st Dec		Continued work on Roads	Sheet France 57c
NEUVILLE BOURJONVAL			(Ref Sheet France 57c)	
Adv H.Qs	2nd Dec		Work carried out on Roads. Regt. Headquarters moved to HERMIES (T 35 Cent) and	Army
- K.15.a.23.				
K.15.a.23	3rd Dec		Coy marched to LE BOUCQUIERE. Casualties 2 killed & 2 wounded	Army
LE BOUCQUIERE	4th Dec		Coy moved at 6 pm to FRÉMICOURT	Army
FRÉMICOURT	5th Dec		3 Sections working in BEUGNY in billets making temporary then	Army
FRÉMICOURT	6th Dec		Coy moved at 9 am to BEUGNY with transport	Army
BEUGNY	7th Dec		2 Sections on Hutting in BEUGNY, also No 2 Sect on Hutting at FRÉMICOURT	Army
"	8th Dec			
"	9th Dec		No 1 & 3 Sect on Hutting in BEUGNY. No 2 Sect at FRÉMICOURT. No 4 Sect	
"	10th Dec		preparing screens. Sect No 4 erect screens at	Remainder as for 9th inst. Army
"	11th Dec		T.17.C. East of BEUGNY.	Army
"	12th Dec		No 1 Sect started Kitchen at T.8.c.4.2. No 2 Sect Hutting in FRÉMICOURT	Army
"	13th Dec		No 3 Sect Huthing in BEUGNY. No 4 Sect Screens at T.12.C.	Army

Army Form C. 2118.

WAR DIARY
or
INTELLIGENCE SUMMARY.
(Erase heading not required.)

Instructions regarding War Diaries and Intelligence Summaries are contained in F. S. Regs., Part II. and the Staff Manual respectively. Title pages will be prepared in manuscript.

Place	Date	Hour	Summary of Events and Information	Remarks and references to Appendices
BEUGNY	14th Dec.		Soup Kitchen started at I.17.d.4.9. Also Hutting in F.24.c.0.7 + 3.6.0.3.a.4.	Sketches 57.3
"	15th Dec.		and screwing at I.17.c. Army	
"	16th Dec.		Soup Kitchen finished. Remainder of work as for 16th Dec. Army	
"	17th Dec.		At 4pm H.Q. Coy transport moved to billets in Sunken road at I.5.c. Army	
"	18th Dec.		Working on SUPPORT LINE. Dugouts & new trench. Also improving billets at T.5.c. Army	
"	19th Dec.		Work done on ROBIN SUPPORT and on SHARK SUPPORT - Digging new trench Army	
"			Work continued on ROBIN SUPPORT and SHARK SUPPORT and on FRONT LINE. Making Cubby holes and digging trenches. Army	
"	20th Dec			
"	21st Dec		Work carried on further as for 19th Dec. Army	
"	22nd Dec			
"	23rd Dec			
"	24th Dec		Work on ROBIN SUPPORT, FRONT LINE, Dugouts, and RABBIT SUPPORT Army	
"	25th Dec		Work on NEW RABBIT SUPPORT. Remainder as for 24th Dec Army	
"	26th Dec		Work as for 25th Dec. Army	
"	27th Dec			

Army Form C. 2118.

WAR DIARY
or
INTELLIGENCE SUMMARY
(Erase heading not required.)

Instructions regarding War Diaries and Intelligence Summaries are contained in F. S. Regs., Part II. and the Staff Manual respectively. Title Pages will be prepared in manuscript.

Place	Date	Hour	Summary of Events and Information	Remarks and references to Appendices
BOVGNY	28th Dec 1917		Working on Robin Support, Rabbit Support, Front Line also Rook Support. Reinforcements - 5 O.R.	A/C
"	29th Dec		Working on Robin Support, New Rabbit Support, Rook Support, Rabbit Alley & Front Line.	PL A
"	30th Dec		Working on Robin Support, Rabbit Support, Rook Support & Front Line. Casualties - 1 O.R.	PL A
"	31st Dec		Working on Robin Support, Rabbit Support, Rabbit Alley, Rook Support & Front Line. Casualties 1 O.R.	A/C

WO 32

CONFIDENTIAL

WAR DIARY

of

404ᵀᴴ (HIGH.) FIELD Cᵒʸ R.E.

FROM 1ˢᵀ TO 31ˢᵀ JANUARY 1918.

WAR DIARY or INTELLIGENCE SUMMARY

Army Form C. 2118.

Place	Date	Hour	Summary of Events and Information	Remarks and references to Appendices
BERGNY Ref. France 57c	JAN 1918			
	1	—	No work — a holiday was observed.	
	2	—	Working on new C.T. from NEW ROBIN SUPPORT to REV 850 yds completed	
	3	—	Do. Do. 230 yds Duckboard	
	4	—	Improving dugouts T.M. Dugout — w/o Bivel sectn to 29th C.C.S.	
	5	—	Working on new CT from ROBIN SUPPORT. Also Dugout	
	6		Work in ROOK ALLEY SUPPORT LINE. Dugout	
	7		Dugouts & shelters at mine craters	
	8		Do	
	9		Working on ROOK ALLEY, ROOK SUPPORT, RABBIT SUPPORT OP & ROBIN SUPPORT	
	10		Working on ROOK Alley drainage & clearing work on SUPPORT LINE on kitchens, latrines & cleaning trench ditto	
	11		ditto	

WAR DIARY or INTELLIGENCE SUMMARY

Army Form C. 2118.

Place	Date	Hour	Summary of Events and Information	Remarks and references to Appendices
BEUNY	12		Working on TOOK ALLEY and on SUPPORT LINE.	
Ref FRANCE SHEET N° 57c	13		ditto	
	14		Working on TOOK ALLEY. Increased strength. Working in SUPPORT LINE. Kitchens, Latrines & Bomb stores. MAJOR PATTINSON arrived to take over the Company.	
	15		Working on TOOK ALLEY & SUPPORT LINE.	
	16		ditto	
	17		ditto	
	18		ditto. Erected two bridges over sewer took	
	19		ALLEY & 1 acres RABBIT ALLEY.	
	20		Company moved from billets in the line to BEUNY.	
COURCELLES-LE-COMTE	21		Company & Transport moved from BEUNY to COURCELLES-LE-COMTE with 153rd Inf. Bgde Group.	
Ref FRANCE (Sheet N° 57)	23		Company started on erection of Nissen hut camp between LOGEAST WOOD and ABLAINZEVILLE.	
	24			
	25		ditto	
	26			
	27			

WAR DIARY
or
INTELLIGENCE SUMMARY
(Erase heading not required.)

Army Form C. 2118.

Instructions regarding War Diaries and Intelligence Summaries are contained in F.S. Regs., Part II. and the Staff Manual respectively. Title Pages will be prepared in manuscript.

Place	Date	Hour	Summary of Events and Information	Remarks and references to Appendices
COURCELLES LE COMTE (Ref FRANCE Sheet N° 57.)	JANUARY 1918 28		4 Sections working on access of frozen huts in camp between LOGEAST WOOD & ABLAINZEVILLE. Draft of 1 N.C.O. & 7 men arrival complete huts in 1 hr. 55 mins. Reinforcements - 3 O.R.s	JR
	29		3 Sections working on another of frozen huts.	JR
RITZ CAMP (Ref G.9.a.5.9.)	30		Company moved to RITZ CAMP (Ref G.9.a.5.9 Sheet 57C) working on erection of Nissen huts, cookhouses, latrines & ablution shed	JR
	31		4 Sections working on Nissen, cookhouses, latrines & ablution shed in RITZ CAMP.	JR

2/2/18

Jae Yeats
Capt
I/c Works FC E(1)
401

CONFIDENTIAL

WAR DIARY

OF

404TH (HIGH) FIELD COY R.E.

Army Form C. 2118.

WAR DIARY
or
INTELLIGENCE SUMMARY
(Erase heading not required.)

Place	Date	Hour	Summary of Events and Information	Remarks and references to Appendices
RITZ CAMP	1st	—	Half Company training. Other half Hutting in RITZ CAMP.	AW
ACHIET-LE-2nd/7th			Day devoted to Hutting and training.	AW
GRAND.	8th		Inspection of Company by the G.O.C. Major Gen. Harper.	AW
	11th		Advance parties proceed forward areas to take over line from 6th Div.	AW
BEUNY	12		Informed billets & repair shops in support line.	
	13		Returning shops in line. GRAYLING SUPPORT tapped out. Reinforcement — 2 O.R's	
	14		75" yards new SUPPORT LINE dug at GRAYLING POST. Work on entrances & O.P tow at new Coy H.Q'rs. Repairing dugouts in line	
	15		Work on dugouts, GRAYLING SUPPORT, dummy STURGEON SUPPORT	
	16		Repairing DEMICOURT-BOISNES ROAD Pillbox — PILL-BOX,	
	17		1 Section started work on new Bgde H.Q'rs on BEAUMETZ-HERMIES Road	O.R
	18		Casualties — 1 O.R. wounded	
	19		Work on DEMICOURT-BOISNES ROAD, STURGEON SUPPORT bomb stores,	
	20		dummy, cleaning French hems, digg GRAYLING SUPPORT.	
	21		Dugouts to line, New Brigade H.Q'rs	
	22		chiefs. Reinforcement — 2 O.R's.	
	23			

Army Form C. 2118.

WAR DIARY
or
INTELLIGENCE SUMMARY

(Erase heading not required.)

Instructions regarding War Diaries and Intelligence Summaries are contained in F. S. Regs., Part II. and the Staff Manual respectively. Title Pages will be prepared in manuscript.

Place	Date	Hour	Summary of Events and Information	Remarks and references to Appendices
BEUGNY	FEB 1918 24		Moving on Nr. Brigade HQ. in BEAUMETZ - HERMIES ROAD. Sub-sections DOIGNES - DEMICOURT ROAD, STURGEON & GRAYAN'S SUPPORT. Shelters 03 sub-parts in lines. Erecting shelters at A.D. Station DOIGNES.	JR JR
	25		Ditto	
	26		Ditto	
	27		Ditto. 2 Sections moved to dugouts near ETLO Central.	JR
	28		LEBUCQUIERE. 2 Sections RE. (Ref France 57c) moved to Sapper Camp.	JR

Capt. R.E.
O.C. Field Coy.
1st Australian Tunnelling Coy.

2/3/18

51st Divisional Engineers

WAR DIARY

404th FIELD COMPANY R. E.

MARCH 1918

WAR DIARY

OF

404th HIGHLAND FIELD COMPANY. R.E.

MARCH 1918.

WARE DIARY
or
INTELLIGENCE SUMMARY.

(Erase heading not required.)

Army Form C. 2118.

Place	Date	Hour	Summary of Events and Information	Remarks and references to Appendices
BEUVRY	MARCH			
trenches 57e	1		2 Sections working on dugouts in FISH AVENUE, CAMBRAI ROAD. M.G. & Scout men DUGOUTS & CUBBY HOLES in FRONT LINE. 1 Section working on Artillery dugouts. 1 Section on Brigade HdQrs and new trestles, A.D.S. at DOIGNIES	JR
	2		Ditto	
	3			
	4			
	5		Ditto	JR
	6			
	7		Reinforcements - 3 o.r.s	
	8			
	11		Ditto	Reinforcements - 1 o.r.
	12		Ditto	- 2 o.r.s. Putting in frames in JR dugout near LEUVERVAL. JR
	21		BEAUMETZ CAVES. Started dugout near LEUVERVAL. German attack. 2 found sections in front line Post. 2 Sections ordered to defend LEBUCQUIÈRE. Reinforcement - 2 o.r.s	JR

WAR DIARY
or
INTELLIGENCE SUMMARY.
(Erase heading not required.)

Army Form C. 2118.

Place	Date	Hour	Summary of Events and Information	Remarks and references to Appendices
	MARCH			
LEBUCQUERE	21		Ren. Hdqrs. moved to advanced postion near DELSAUX FARM	JR
			LIEUT. ALLAN & TELFORD wounded 1 O.R killed. 30 O.Rs wounded 30 O.Rs missing	JR
	22		Heavy enemy shelling near BEAUMETZ and LEBUCQUERE	JR
			Transport moved to further outskirts of BAPAUME. Left flank	JR
			of our Line at position formed defensive flank intact.	JR
			LEBUCQUERE.	JR
GREVILLERS	23		Enemy attack. Left flank gave position. Withdrew to VELU	JR
			Line. Casualties - 1 O.R. wounded.	JR
MIRAMONT	24		2 Sections from BANCOURT LINE 2 Platoons near BAPAUME	JR
			Coulter - 1 O.R. wounded	JR
FORCEVILLE	25		Attack on BANCOURT LINE and BAPAUME-Coulter-	JR
			LIEUT ROBERTSON Killed 6 O.R.s wounded	JR
SOUASTRE	26		Attack on TILLOY and IRLES LINE Coulter - 30 O.Rs wounded - 60 O.Rs missing	JR
	27		Confn. moved from SOUASTRE to PAS	JR
NEUVILLETTE	27		Confn. moved from PAS to NEUVILLETTE.	JR
FOUQUIERES	29		Confn. moved from NEUVILLETTE to FOUQUIERES. JRae Capt.	JR
			Adjutant Sect. C. R.E.M	
			40th	

51st Divisional Engineers

WAR DIARY

404th (Highland) FIELD COMPANY R. E.

APRIL 1 9 1 8

WAR DIARY

OF

404TH HIGHLAND FIELD COY R.E.

APRIL 1918.

WAR DIARY

OF

404ᵀᴴ HIGHLAND FIELD COY R.E.

APRIL 1918.

WAR DIARY
or
INTELLIGENCE SUMMARY.
(Erase heading not required.)

Army Form C. 2118.

Place	Date	Hour	Summary of Events and Information	Remarks and references to Appendices
FOUQUIERES (Ref HAZEBROUCK 5A)	APRIL 1		Parado. Reorganing. Confort.	
			Reinforcements – 1 Off + 14 ORs.	JR
CAMBLAIN-CHATELAIN	4		Company moved to CAMBLAIN-CHATELAIN. (Ref LENS 11)	JR
CANTRAINE (Ref HAZEBROUCK 5A)	5		Company moved to CANTRAINE (Ref HAZEBROUCK 5A). Reinforcements – 2 Off + 40 ORs.	JR JR
	6		Company Parade – drills etc.	JR
L'ECLEME.	7		Company moved to L'ECLEME (Ref HAZEBROUCK 5A) Heavy German attack on front.	JR
	9		Company "stood to". 6 Co. & Lt WALLACE & Lt CAMERON / Reconnoitre bridges for demolition across some ENNERIN river VIEILLE CHAPELLE (France 28A) Lt WALLACE DIOR. stay with Sappers in line. Heavy attack on VIEILLE CHAPELLE at night – loss of 10R. others.	JR
	10		Company ordered into line with 152 Inf Brigade. Take up posts in front of LE CORNET MALO – 3 Posters in two @ 1 in reserve. Hq. in	JR
	11		Chapel. moved back to LE CORNET BOURDOIS with 152 Brigade. Took up line attack on front. Hy. Bohn. almost surrounded. H.Q. got out. German attack on front.	JR
	12		Took up line along BASSEE CANAL about 735. 36. 931. (Ref France 36A) Drawbridge prepared for demolition. 3 Bridges destroyed + rear covered part day to help withdrawal of French Artillery & transport. Counterattack – 2 OR killed Huy to transport. Moved to FONTES. (Ref HAZEBROUCK 5A).	JR JR
				= 1 OR wounded
				= 1 OR wounded prisoner JR
				= 1 OFF + 30 ORs missing JR

Army Form C. 2118.

WAR DIARY
or
INTELLIGENCE SUMMARY.
(Erase heading not required.)

Instructions regarding War Diaries and Intelligence Summaries are contained in F. S. Regs., Part II. and the Staff Manual respectively. Title pages will be prepared in manuscript.

Place	Date	Hour	Summary of Events and Information	Remarks and references to Appendices
BUSNES (Ref. France 36A)	13		Company moved into billets in BUSNES.	A
	14		Company all out all night putting up wire in front of ROBECQ about P.30. (France 36A).	A
HAM-EN-ARTOIS (Ref. HAZEBROUCK 5A)	15		Company moved to HAM-EN-ARTOIS (Ref. HAZEBROUCK 5A) Transport remained at	A
	16.		FONTES. 2 sections erected huts bridge for tanks at I.35.a.3.8.	A
	17		Section framing. Billets etc.	A
ST. HILAIRE (Ref. HAZEBROUCK 5A)	22		Company moved to ST. HILAIRE and took over billets & own posts from Company R.E.	
FONTES (Ref. France 36A)	24		Company moved to P.27.a.77 and took over from P.29.74. P.84.B.8.0. 1 Section on bridges at P.29.c.73 P.29.71 P.23.4.2. 40.4.04. Co R.E. 1 Section on bridges being prepared for demolition on LES AMUSÉES (P.17 out) to LA BASSEE CANAL 1200 west of ROBECQ. Coy being joined under orders of C.R.E. 61st Division. 1 Section framing I Hut for transport moved to FONTES.	A
	25		ditto.	A

Army Form C. 2118.

WAR DIARY
or
INTELLIGENCE SUMMARY.
(Erase heading not required.)

Instructions regarding War Diaries and Intelligence Summaries are contained in F. S. Regs., Part II. and the Staff Manual respectively. Title pages will be prepared in manuscript.

Place	Date	Hour	Summary of Events and Information	Remarks and references to Appendices
FONTES (Ref France 3A)	APRIL 26		1 Section on Bridge at P.29.a.73. P.23.d.42. P.29.7.74. P.24.3.80. + P.29.a.71. Clear Bridges are prepared for demolition. 3 Sections from R.E. sent up to LINE from LES AMUSOIRES to LA BASSÉE CANAL 1200 west of ROBECQ. Coy HQ working under orders of O.C.E. 61st Division.	
	27		ditto	
	28		ditto	Casualties – 1 OR wounded
	29		ditto	Reinforcements – 4 ORs from workshop
	30		ditto	Casualties – 1 OR wounded

CONFIDENTIAL.

WAR DIARY for MAY, 1918.

of the

404th (HIGHLAND) FIELD COMPANY. R.E.

WAR DIARY or INTELLIGENCE SUMMARY

Army Form C. 2118.

Place	Date	Hour	Summary of Events and Information	Remarks and references to Appendices
FONTES (Ref. Thames 36c)	May 1		3 Platoons work on SWITCH LINE from LES AMUSOIRS to LA BASSÉE CANAL 1200 yds West of ROBECQ. (Details on Bridges at P.29.c.7.3. P.23.d.1.2. P.29.b.7.4, P.24.8.0, P.29.71) These bridges are prepared for demolition. Billet hard, installed during the night. 1 O.R. wounded, Canadian. 1 O.R. wounded, 1 killed.	
	2		Company working as above. At NAPIER LINE transferred from 400 to 425 R.E. to I.R.	
	3		Company moved from ROBECQ to billet in LAMBRES, reinforcement - 10 O.R.	
	4		Company moved (to the orders of 153 Inf. Bde.) to DIVN. Transport moved by Bois DE BRAY (LENS II) & C. Bois Nancy.	
(Ref LENS II)	5		From AIRE (HAZEBROUCK S.A.) to A.9 (LENS II) and reached from the camp in BOIS DE BRAY (Ref LENS II)	
	6		Took over work (from 127 Fd. Co. R.E.) Two Platoons moved to form Billets at B.20.d (28. Canada Camp) & 9 Fd. Co. transferred from work	
AUX REITZ (Ref MARQUELUA SHEET)	7		to AUX REITZ A.8.c.5.7. 2 Platoons moved & transferred to camp at A.0.70.8.7. Two Platoons working on OUSE ALLEY.	
	8		2 Platoons working on OUSE ALLEY. 1 Platoon work on dugouts in TUNNEL. 1 Platoon improving camp	
	9		2 Platoons moved to billets in Railway cutting at B.26.B.5.1, after a week on OUSE ALLEY.	

WAR DIARY or INTELLIGENCE SUMMARY

Army Form C. 2118.

Place	Date	Hour	Summary of Events and Information	Remarks and references to Appendices
A27 & 87 (MARŒUIL SHEET)	MAY 10		2 Forward Sections finishing TOMMY TRENCH Dugout and revetting shelters and blew up Stink. 1 Section working on dugout in TUNNEL.	
	11		DITTO	
	12		DITTO	
	13		2 Sections moved forward to Billets in Railway Cutting. 2 Sections out on work digging POST LINE with 2nd/1st work party.	
			2 Sections out digging SS front line with 2nd/1st work party.	
	14		ditto	
	15		1 Section digging Post Line on the Def. work party. 1 Section work on new Comm. trench. 1 Section working on Def. POST LINE. 1.2 Section digging new Comm. Trench with 2nd/1st work party.	
	16			
	17		2 Sections digging new front line with Inf work party. 2 Sections relieved by 2 Sections of 2nd/4th Highland Field Co. R.E. & Section relieved by Billets in MARŒUIL. Remainder. 2nd 1st moved to Billets in MARŒUIL.	
MARŒUIL	18		1 Section work on survivors Hqrs. 1 Section work at Divisional School. Bois DE BRAY. Remainder of Coy on Baths. Relieved by 4th Highland Field Co R.E. and moved to Billets.	

in MARŒUIL.

Army Form C. 2118.

WAR DIARY
or
INTELLIGENCE SUMMARY.
(Erase heading not required.)

Instructions regarding War Diaries and Intelligence Summaries are contained in F. S. Regs., Part II. and the Staff Manual respectively. Title pages will be prepared in manuscript.

Place	Date	Hour	Summary of Events and Information	Remarks and references to Appendices
MARDEUIL	MAY 1918 20		1 Section moved forward to billets at B.26.0.6. 1 Section to billets at B.20.6.	
	21		2.1. for work on POST LINE. 1 Section party on DIV HDQRS	
	21		1 Section work on DIV. SCHOOL	
	22		2 Sections work on POST LINE with Inf. working party. Digging and widening trench. work also started on 3 dugouts. Electric	
	23		light on DIV HDQRS. 1 Section on DIV SCHOOL fitting up Dining Hall	
	24		and Lecture Room.	
			Reinforcements 23/5/18 — 3 O.R's	
			4727 Smith (for 2nd front line.	
	25		2 front sections on post line with Inf. W.P. & 4 dugouts. 1 Section on Div H.Q. 1 section W.P.	
	26		on Divl. School. 7 O.R. join 2d 26.5.18.	
	27			
	28		2 front sections on post line etc. 1 rear section on soda water factory at AUBIGNY. W.P.	
	29		1 Rear Section training etc	
	30			
	31			

WR Hn
OC MT
OC 447th (A) Fd Coy RE

WAR DIARY

of

404 (HIGH) FIELD COY R.E.

JUNE 1918.

WAR DIARY or INTELLIGENCE SUMMARY

Army Form C. 2118.

(Erase heading not required.)

Place	Date	Hour	Summary of Events and Information	Remarks and references to Appendices
MARŒUIL SHEET (MARŒUIL)	JUNE 1		2 Forward Picket work on POST LINE with Lt. Bolton. Working party of 400 men under 4 Officers to Kneller trench. Also working on 1 dugout at POST LINE 6, 3 dugouts at Kneller trench at BROWN LINE. 1 Sea forth was guard on Kola Factory AUBIGNY. 1 Section Granny.	J.R.
	2		Ditto	J.R.
	3		Ditto. Kola factory completed except for machines.	J.R.
	4		Ditto — Reinforcement — 1 O.R.	J.R.
	5		Ditto —	
	6		2 Forward picket work on POST LINE & on Dugouts. Casualty — 1 O.R. wounded	J.R.
	7		2 Sea forths Granny	
	8		1 Forward picket work on BROWN LINE with 2 Sections Granny looking party from TOMMY ALLEY northwards, making dugouts & knocking 2 trench, also work on 1 dugout in POST LINE, 1 Dugout BROWN LINE DIMG enforcement at GABLE HOUSE BAILLEUL. Forward section on work party (widening dugouts) MISSISSIPPI trench north of Quesh at & BROWN LINE @ 1 M.G. Quesh trench, also in work on 2 dugouts at BROWN LINE & Sea Forth Granny.	J.R.
	9		Enfilade at B.22.6.7.5. @ Sea forth Granny	J.R.
	10			
	11		Ditto	
	12			
	13		Ditto	
	14			
	15			
	16			
	17			
	18			
	19			
	20			
	21			
	22			
	23			

Army Form C. 2118.

WAR DIARY
or
INTELLIGENCE SUMMARY.
(Erase heading not required.)

Instructions regarding War Diaries and Intelligence Summaries are contained in F. S. Regs., Part II. and the Staff Manual respectively. Title pages will be prepared in manuscript.

Place	Date	Hour	Summary of Events and Information	Remarks and references to Appendices
MAROEUIL (Ref Sheet MAROEUIL)	JUNE 21		1 Forward Section work on BROWN LINE with 2nd Works Party from TRENCH mortars, making dugouts, deepening & finishing trench, also work on dugout POST LINE & 1 Sgt on BROWN LINE. 6 I.M.S. enfilade at GABLE HOUSE, BAILLEUL. 1 Reserve Section work on MISSISSIPPI TRENCH mortars with 2nd works party, making deepening & finishing trench, also work on 2 dugouts in BROWN LINE & 1 M.G. emplacement at 32.22.75. 2 Res Sections training.	
	22		Ditto	
	23		Ditto	Reinforcements — 30 ORs
	24		Ditto	
	25		Ditto	
	26			
	27		Forward Section work on BROWN LINE and one 5 dugouts. Res Section working at Gun School.	
	28		Ditto	
	29		Ditto	Casualty — 1 OR wounded
	30			

Divisional Engineers.

51st (Highland) Division.

404th FIELD CO., R. E.

JULY, 1918.

WR38

War Diary

of

404th Highland Field Company R.E.

July 1918.

Confidential

WAR DIARY or INTELLIGENCE SUMMARY

Army Form C. 2118.

Place	Date 1918 JULY	Hour	Summary of Events and Information	Remarks and references to Appendices
MAREUIL Ref.(MAREUIL)	1		3 forward Sections working on BROWN LINE, water & defence. Rest of D on S.Dg.A.1. Rear Section working on Div. School	
	2,3,4,5,6,7,8		Ditto	
	9		Ditto	
	10		All company went take over 9, 10th Canadian Batt. C.E.4 h Div. Sections concentrate at MAREUIL. Reinforcements – 1 O.R.	
	11		Company entrained near ECURIE for DIGVAL checked from there to billets in BEUGIN. Transport moved by road.	
BEUGIN (Rd. of LENS 11)	12,13,15,16		Return training.	
	16		Company & Transport entrained at PERNES 5 a.m. detrained at PONT-SUR-SEINE. Transport moved by road to FONTAINE-ST-DENIS.	
MOUSSY (Rd. Rhet. of CHALONS)	17		Sections moved by bus to MOUSSY	
	18		Transport arrived at MOUSSY all 62nd Div. Sections & Fields also 51st Div. Sections & Staples concentrated at MOUSSY. Company detailed for work under 5th French Army Cav. Corps.	
	19		Company moved with Cav. Corps to RAMPONNEAU, made orders for CRE of Cav. Corps	
RAMPONNEAU	20			
	21		Company standing by marking orders	

WAR DIARY
or
INTELLIGENCE SUMMARY.

Army Form C. 2118.

Place	Date	Hour	Summary of Events and Information	Remarks and references to Appendices
RAMTONNEAU Ref (Oct CHALONS)	JULY 1918 22		Company standing to await orders from 14th French Corps.	
	25		5th Army. Orders - Casualty - 1 O.R. wounded. For orders to march to IGNY-LE-JARD. (East CHALONS)	
IGNY-LE-JARD	26		Tack on prepared pontoon Bridge. Reconnoitred Bridge across the River MARNE N.E. of TROISSY.	
	27		For orders at 8/12 noon. Company constructed pontoon & trestle bridge across River MARNE near TROISSY.	
	28		2 Sections working on repairs of pontoon bridge.	
	~~29~~ 31		Company moved to billets in TROISSY. Company dismantled pontoon bridge during the journey.	

5/8/18

CONFIDENTIAL.

Vol 39

WAR DIARY.

OF.

404TH HIGHLAND FIELD COMPANY R.E.

AUGUST 1918.

WAR DIARY
or
INTELLIGENCE SUMMARY.
(Erase heading not required.)

Army Form C. 2118.

Place	Date 1918	Hour	Summary of Events and Information	Remarks and references to Appendices
MOUSSY Rfy. Stat. (CHALONS)	August 1		Company moved to billets at MOUSSY	
	2		Company left at 9.30 pm to entrain at OISY STATION	
	3		Entrained at 3.30 a.m.	
	4		Company detrained at BRIAS (Rly.stat. LENS II) and marched to billets in CAUCOURT	
CAUCOURT Rfy (LENS II)	5		Company training	
	6			
	7		ditto	
	8		ditto	
	9		ditto	
	10			
	11			
	12			
	13			Reinforcement - 8 O.R.s
	14			
	15			Reinforcement - 3 O.R.s
	16			Reinforcement - 1 O.R.
	17			
	18			
	19		Transport moved by road to billets in LOUEZ CAUCHIE. Detrained at ANZIN and marched to billets at G.18.a.8.2. 1 Section standing to under orders of B.G.C. 152nd Inf Brigade	
LOUEZ Rfy Stat (LENS II)	20		1 Section attached to 152nd Brigade. 2 Sections erect bomb store & shelters	
	21		1 Section in charge of demolition scheme in Brigade area. Reinforcement - 5 O.R.s	
	22		ditto	
	23		1 Section in charge of demolition scheme. 2 Sections erecting shelters. 1 Section work with M. Bge Co. Casualties - 1 O.R. wounded	

Army Form C. 2118.

WAR DIARY
or
INTELLIGENCE SUMMARY.
(Erase heading not required.)

Instructions regarding War Diaries and Intelligence Summaries are contained in F. S. Regs., Part II. and the Staff Manual respectively. Title pages will be prepared in manuscript.

Place	Date 1918	Hour	Summary of Events and Information	Remarks and references to Appendices
LOOSE R/(West LENS))	AUGUST 24		1 Section attached to Brigade. 1 Section in charge of demolition scheme in Brigade area. 2 Sections erecting huts stores & shelters	J.F.
	25		ditto	J.F.
	26		Casualties - 8 O.R.s wounded (gas) near SCARPE near FAMPOUX.	J.F.
			Company Build two pontoon bridges across river SCARPE near FAMPOUX. 1 Section attached to Artillery Brigade	J.F.
	27		Casualties - 4 O.R.s wounded (gas) [gassed?] on rd BLANGY-FAMPOUX road. 1 Section attached 2" north Artillery Brigade	J.F.
	28		ditto	
	29		ditto	
	30		ditto Transport moved to billets at	J.F.
	31		G.8.c.7.7. ANZIN.	

Ac. Capt. CO
1st Field Co
4th Highland R.E. (T)
1/9/18

CONFIDENTIAL

WAR DIARY
OF
404 HIGH. FIELD COMPANY
R.E.

SEPTEMBER. 1918.

WAR DIARY
or
INTELLIGENCE SUMMARY.

Army Form C. 2118.

Place	Date	Hour	Summary of Events and Information	Remarks and references to Appendices
ANZIN Rd (LENS II)	SEPT. 1		Officers & advanced headquarters moved to Billets in PUDDING TRENCH at H.16.b. (Trench sheet 51.B N.W.) 2 Sections clearing channel of River SCARPE where Railway bridge at H.24.a.47. was destroyed. 1 Section on Brigade Hqrs. erecting shelters. 1 Section dismantled bath houses at ST CATHERINE	R.E.P.
	2		2 Sections clearing debris at RAILWAY BRIDGE H 24.a.4.7. 2 Sections working on Inf. Brigade Hqr. & Art Brigade Hqr. erecting shelters	R.E.P.
	3		1 Section clearing debris at Railway Bridge. 1 Section with I.O. workshop started digging new line of trestles east of HAUSA WOOD. 1 Section working on Inf. Brigade Hqrs. 1 Section dismantling destroyed enemy Bridge at ROEUX I 19.d.9.8.	R.E.P.
	4		ditto	R.E.P.
	5 6 7 8 9		1 Section drawing SCARPE VALLEY between FAMPOUX & ROEUX. 1 Section digging path & working party, dealing with our return of resistance east of HAUSA WOOD R.E.P. our return erecting shelter bridges – 60 m. Horse transport ROEUX I.18.d.1.1 our Return – Pullens BRIGADE Hq. I.17.16.a.95.80 Pontoons 1.02. 9th Septm 8.15.a	R.E.P.
	10 11 12		1 Section salvaging R.E. stores & forming advanced DUMP I.20.a.95.25. and erecting BATH HOUSE H.18.d.8.8. 2 Sections erecting trestle bridge – ROEUX I.19.d.8.2.8. 400x east of trestle bridge. – 1 Section making Pullens Brigade HQ + repairing footbridge	R.E.P.
	13		Company moved from ANZIN to "LE PENDU CAMP. Ref Army Map "C" X.25.c.4.2	R.E.P.

Army Form C. 2118.

WAR DIARY
or
INTELLIGENCE SUMMARY.
(Erase heading not required.)

Instructions regarding War Diaries and Intelligence Summaries are contained in F. S. Regs., Part II. and the Staff Manual respectively. Title pages will be prepared in manuscript.

Place	Date	Hour	Summary of Events and Information	Remarks and references to Appendices
LE PENDU CAMP	SEPT. 14		Company training –	R.R.P
	15		Ditto ditto	R.R.P
Ref. Army Map "C"	16		Reinforcements 1D 6R –	R.R.P
X.25.c.4.2.	17		Reinforcements 2 6R –	R.R.P
	18		Company training –	R.R.P.
	19		Company training –	R.R.P.
	19		Company training.	R.R.P.
	20		Company training –	R.R.P.
	21		Company training –	R.R.P.
	22		Company training –	R.R.P
	23		Company moved from LE PENDU CAMP to ANZIN – 2 R.R.P. 2 Return Rothen & Adv. H.Q. 15	R.R.P
ANZIN (Ref. LENS 11)			PUDDING TRENCH – H.16.b. (Trench 51B. N.W.) 2 Sections at Rear H.Q. 2 Returns forward – 2 Sections standing by to	R.R.P
	24		make up DUMMIES for proposed CHINESE ATTACK. – 9 Reinforcements	R.R.P
	25		2 Rear Returns making up "DUMMIES" 2 forward Returns upon of BILLETS forward Return to Rear H.Q. 15 attend demonstration & return	R.R.P
	26		PUDDING TRENCH. Firing "DUMMIES" 1.9.b. – 1.10.c. (51B N.W.) 4 Sections at in front of Battes ROUVAIN – 1 N.C.O wounded 1 O.R. wounded –	R.R.P

Army Form C. 2118.

WAR DIARY
or
INTELLIGENCE SUMMARY.
(Erase heading not required.)

Instructions regarding War Diaries and Intelligence Summaries are contained in F. S. Regs., Part II. and the Staff Manual respectively. Title pages will be prepared in manuscript.

Place	Date	Hour	Summary of Events and Information	Remarks and references to Appendices
ANZIN. (Rf LENS 11)	Sept. 27		1 Section to Rear HQ. 2 Sections obtaining ROEUX - PLOUVAIN ROAD. Laying cables when at Returning. Reknowing TQE materiel at BANKS of SCARPE - Work at Bde HQrs	RMP RMP RMP
	28		ditto ditto ditto	RMP
	29		ditto ditto ditto	RMP
	30		Classes BRAY (LENS II) preparing to proceed 1 N.O. to move to DIVISION as near to Adrian Huts.	RMP

R.L. Peters (?) B-RCD
Lieut. Highland Field Coy RE

CONFIDENTIAL.

Vol 4

WAR DIARY
of
404th (HIGH) FIELD Coy R.E.
FOR OCT. 1918.

WAR DIARY or INTELLIGENCE SUMMARY

Army Form C. 2118.

Place	Date	Hour	Summary of Events and Information	Remarks and references to Appendices
ANZIN (LENS 11)	Oct. 1		Forward H.Q. PUDDING TRENCH - H.16.b (FRANCE 51B N.W.) Rear H.Q. TRANSPORT LINES G.6.C.7.7. - (FRANCE 51B N.W.) 3 Sections forward. 1 Section at Rear H.Q.	P of M P
	2		2 Sections preparing ROEUX - PLOUVAIN ROAD.	P of M P
	3 to 6		1 Section returning RE. material to BANKER of SCARPE.	P of M P
			BDE. H.Q.	P of M P
	6		N.C.O. to view Rear Sections at BRAY (LENS 11) preparation of Huts at	P of M P
	7 8		DIVISIONAL CLASSES.	
Sheet 57c BRAY (LENS 11)			Also distrib by H.Q. Field Coy. Company moved to BRAY. -	P of M P
			Relieved Company training - Reinforcements 1 N.C.O.	
Ref FRANCE 57c C.6.b.			Company Training -	
			Moved to QUEANT Area -	
			QUEANT Area.	
Ref FRANCE 57c F.15.a.4.6	10		Moved to SAND PIT - FONTAINE NOTRE DAME.	P of M P
Ref 51.A.3.w. T.20.d central	11		Moved to T.20.d central	P of M P
	12		Worked out Assembly positions for attacks	P of M P
T.6.C.5.75	13		Moved to IWUY - T.6.C.5.75 - Transport at T.11.b.2.6. One Section attached 152 Brigade	P of M P
T.10.d central	14		Moved to T.10.d central	P of M P
	15		Standing by to bridge RIVER SELLE	P of M P
	16		One Section worked for 152 Brigade.	P of M P
	17		One Section at Brigade H.Q. T.3.C.9.7.	P of M P
	18		One Section making diversion at THUN - IWUY Road. -	P of M P

Army Form C. 2118.

WAR DIARY
or
INTELLIGENCE SUMMARY.
(Erase heading not required.)

Instructions regarding War Diaries and Intelligence Summaries are contained in F. S. Regs., Part II. and the Staff Manual respectively. Title pages will be prepared in manuscript.

Place	Date	Hour	Summary of Events and Information	Remarks and references to Appendices
SHEET 51a T.10.d central	Oct 19		Reconnaissance of RIVER SELLE - evening. Commenced indexing night 1.35 a.	R&P
AVESNES LE SEC	20		Move to AVESNES LE SEC - Bridge on RIVER SELLE at FLEURY. O.L.a.	R&P
	21		7 OR Reinforced.	R&P
	22		Our recce maintaining approaches to Bridge.	R&P
	23		Reconnaissance of Roads & Bridges to THIANT.	R&P
	24		Two Bridges on RIVER ECAILLON J.27.d.1.7. at THIANT. 2 OR wounded (minimum water) Mars 15 DOUCHY.	R&P
DOUCHY	25		One Bridge on ECAILLON (improved water) J.27.d.65.25. 1 Officer	R&P
	26		Bridge on ECAILLON. Our forward at THIANT & THIANT AREA.	R&P
	27		Reconnaissance of ECAILLON at J.21.d.7.4.	R&P
	28		Bridge for 60 m. Completed. 60 m Bridge.	R&P
	29		Both helps in BOSSEVILLE.	R&P
51.a.S.W. PAILLENCOURT N.19.a.95.25	30		Company cleaning up.	R&P
	31		Company moved to N.19.a.95.25. PAILLENCOURT.	R&P

B.M. Palmer Lt
M.C.(?) Field Coy Re

(6339) Wt. W160/M3016 1,500,000 10/17 McA & W Ltd (E 1898) Forms W3091.   Army Form W.3091.

Cover for Documents.

Nature of Enclosures.

WAR DIARY

OF

404th (HIGH) FIELD COY. R.E.

FOR

NOVEMBER 1918.

Notes, or Letters written.

WAR DIARY
or
INTELLIGENCE SUMMARY.

Army Form C. 2118.

Place	Date	Hour	Summary of Events and Information	Remarks and references to Appendices
51A. S.W. PALLENCOURT. N.19.a.95.25.	Jan-1918			
	1st		Company generally cleaning up, magns dryg etc. Box Respirators fitted by Gas Officer.	
	2nd		Inspection of O.C. Reconnaissance of Battle Posn at HORDAIN.	
	3rd		Company with Lt. SMITH moved to INCHY & saw Battn. - Church Parade - 1 N.C.O & 3 men infantry Battn at HORDAIN.	
	4th		Sectn 1 + 2 squad training as per programme. Sectn 3 work with 152 Inf Bde at THUN-LEVEQUE & THUN-ST.MARTIN - infantry Bridge etc - Sectn 4 working at INCHY Dugs making target for 153 Inf Bde.	
	5th		Sectn 1 + 2 Training. Sectn 3. Working with 152 Inf Bde. Sectn 4 Rigging targets at INCHY. Working Targets & Infantry working party at Rifle Range at N.28.a. 27 - N.28.a. 1.7. Scout Officer & Senior N.C.Os reconn. roads from PALLENCOURT & WAMISS au Bac.	
	6th		Sectn 1 + 2 Training. Sectn 3 working with 152 Inf Bde. Sectn 4 1 N.C.O & 2 men making Target for M.G. Bats at INCHY - avoidable Training. 2nd Lt. Watson.	
	7th		Do Do Do. 2nd Lt. WATSON reconn. & also inspect the German Bartyne Line.	
	8th		Sectn 1, 2 + 4 Training history etc. Lt. PATON with 5 men from Sectn 3 formed AUBIGNY to dismantle Sodr Water Factory - remarks that 3 men 153 Inf Bde.	

WAR DIARY
or
INTELLIGENCE SUMMARY.
(Erase heading not required.)

Army Form C. 2118.

Place	Date	Hour	Summary of Events and Information	Remarks and references to Appendices
St. SW	Nov 1918			
PAILLENCOURT N.19.a.95.25.	9th	9am	Sections 1,2,3,4 at Rifle Range. At PATERSON fort at AUBIGNY - remainder of Coy 3 except section 5 & 2 Pls. Regl. at C - 28. Battalion Fatigue Parades.	GB
	10th		Sections 1,2 & 4 Training - bridging work, topography & knots. Yesterday 5,3 & 152 Inf. Bde. Saker Officers from N.C.O.s make reconnaissance of Bridges as far Schelm by C.C.	GB
	11th	12	General Holiday. ARMISTICE declared as from 11.00 hrs today	GB
VALENCIENNES 1/100,000	12th		Company move to NEUVILLE ST. REMY.	GB
NEUVILLE ST. REMY	13th		Company Training as per programme	GB
A.C.65.25.	14th		Sections 1,2,3,4 working on refreshment waggons. Clearing & painting Company waggons	GB
	15th		Company Training as per programme	GB
	16th			GB
	17th		R.E. Sports at PAILLENCOURT	GB
	18th		Inspection by Divisional General. - Inspection of waggons by I.O.M.	GB
	19th		Company Training as per programme	GB
	20th		do	GB
	21st		No. 1 Section commenced work on Bridgehead at ESCAUDOEUVRES. - 2,3,4. Sections Training	GB
	22nd		do	GB
	23rd		do	GB
	24th		No. 1 Section completed Bridgehead. No. 2,3 work on Rifle Range No. 4 Sec. cleaning bassy area	GB

Army Form C. 2118.

WAR DIARY
or
INTELLIGENCE SUMMARY.
(Erase heading not required.)

Place	Date	Hour	Summary of Events and Information	Remarks and references to Appendices
	Nov 1918			
VALENCIENNES.	25th		Company went to ESCADOEUVRES for Baths	JB
1/100,000. NEUVILLE ST. REMY.	26th 27th 28th 29th		Company Training and fatigues	JB JB
4.C.65.25.	30		Company found & moved to Denain and Shot Ground near THUN-LEVEQUE	JB

J. Boyd
Capt. R.E.
for O.C. 409th (N.M.) Field Co. R.E.

WAR DIARY

OF

404TH (H) FIELD COY RE

FOR

DECEMBER 1918.

Army Form C. 2118.

WAR DIARY
or
INTELLIGENCE SUMMARY.
(Erase heading not required.)

Instructions regarding War Diaries and Intelligence Summaries are contained in F. S. Regs., Part II. and the Staff Manual respectively. Title pages will be prepared in manuscript.

Place	Date 1916 December	Hour	Summary of Events and Information	Remarks and references to Appendices
FRANCE VALENCIENNES 4.C.60.25	1			R.W.P
	2			R.W.P
	3		Church service	
	4			R.W.P
	5			
	6		Company training and sports.	
	7			
	8			R.W.P
	9		Church service.	
	10			R.W.P
	11			
	12		Company training and sports	
	13			
	14			R.W.P
	15		Church service.	
	16			R.W.P
	17			
	18		Company training and sports	
	19			
	20			R.W.P
	21		Church service.	R.W.P
	22		Company training and sports.	R.W.P
	23			
	24		Holiday	
	25			R.W.P
	26		Company training — Schemes of "Being" shelled in trees	
	27			
	28			R.W.P
	29			R.W.P
	30			
	31			

R.W.Ralph Lt. Col. O/C 1st Bn.
1st/4th Highland Light Infy.

CONFIDENTIAL

WAR DIARY

of

404th (HIGH.) FIELD COY R.E.

FOR

JANUARY 1919

Army Form C. 2118.

WAR DIARY
or
INTELLIGENCE SUMMARY.
(Erase heading not required.)

Instructions regarding War Diaries and Intelligence Summaries are contained in F. S. Regs., Part II. and the Staff Manual respectively. Title pages will be prepared in manuscript.

Place	Date	Hour	Summary of Events and Information	Remarks and references to Appendices
NEVILLE-ST.	JAN. 1		Holiday	
REMY	2		1 Recruit on demand of 2nd Bath. in Brigade area	
	3		3 Recruits Joined. 2 Returns moved to HOUDENG-AMERIE by bus (Bef. about BELGIUM) 46.	
	4		Church Service	
hq dep -	5			
VALENCIENNES	6			
	7		Training & Sports Programme	
1/9000	8			
4.C.65.25	9			
	10		Reinforcements – 3 O.R's.	
	11		Reinforcements – 4 O.R's.	
	12		Confer. Transport moved to FAMARS (district VALENCIENNES)	
	13		Confer. Transport moved to JEMAPPES. Branded proved embraced at FAUBERG ST. ROCH and moved to HOUDENG-AMERIE (Bef. BELGIUM - Sheet 46. B172.45)	
	14		Confer. Transport arrived at HOUDENG-AMERIE.	
	15		4 destin working on improvement in 152 Inf. Brigade area, shaking corkscrew pickets etc.	
	16			
	17			
	18		Reinforcement – 1 O.R.	
	19		Church Service	
	20			
	21		3 destin working in Brigade area	
	22		Reinforcement – 10 FF.	
	23		1 destin France	
	24			
	25			
	26		Church Service	
	27		Confer. working – Brigade area	
	28			
	29			
	30			
	31		3 Nissen Huts erected.	

WAR DIARY Vol 45

of

404TH (HIGH) FIELD COY RE

FOR

FEBRUARY 1919.

CONFIDENTIAL

Army Form C. 2118.

WAR DIARY
or
INTELLIGENCE SUMMARY.

(Erase heading not required.)

Instructions regarding War Diaries and Intelligence Summaries are contained in F. S. Regs., Part II. and the Staff Manual respectively. Title pages will be prepared in manuscript.

Place	Date	Hour	Summary of Events and Information	Remarks and references to Appendices
HOUDENG AMERIE	FEB. 1		Company work in Brigade area. Enacting ovens and cookhouse plates	
	2		Church Parade	
Ref Valenciennes 1/100,000 4.C.65.25	3			Reinforcement - 1 O.R.
	4		2 Sections working in Brigade area.	
	5		2 Sections drill & training	
	6			
	7			
	8		Church Parade	
	9			
	10		2 Sections working in Brigade area	
	11		2 Sections drill & training	
	12			
	13			
	14			
	15		Oporto	
	16			
	17		3 Nissen Huts & 1 Universal Hut dismantled in Brigade area.	
	18		Remainder of company drill & training.	
	19			
	20			
	21			
	22		Church Parade	
	23			
	24		Sappers engaged in overhauling & cleaning all company equipment.	
	25		Oporto in afternoon.	
	26			
	27			
	28		During the month 3 Officers and 84 O.R.s were sent to U.K. for demobilization	

9/3/19
[signature]
O.C. 110 Co
R.E.

Wal 46

CONFIDENTIAL

WAR DIARY
OF
404TH (HIGH) FIELD COY RE
FOR
MARCH 1919

Army Form C. 2118.

WAR DIARY
or
INTELLIGENCE SUMMARY.
(Erase heading not required.)

Instructions regarding War Diaries and Intelligence Summaries are contained in F. S. Regs., Part II. and the Staff Manual respectively. Title pages will be prepared in manuscript.

Place	Date	Hour	Summary of Events and Information	Remarks and references to Appendices
HOUDENG- AMERIE Rd BELGIUM Sheet 46.	MARCH 1 2 3 4 5 6 7 8 9 10 11 12 13 14 15		Company employed on checking of equipment, on guards & fatigues & on company stores & on passes &c.	
	16 17 18 19 20	08.15	Left for Army on the Rhine. 64th Field Co. R.E.	
MANAGE Rd BELGIUM Sheet 46	21 22 23 24 25 26 27 28 29 30 31		Company Cadre Established, retired from Cadre 3 to Cadre A 1 Off. O/R to Army on the Rhine. 209 N/Field Co R.E. Company (with transport minus 16 Plcts) in MANAGE (Sheet 46 BELGIUM) Company employed on guards & fatigues & fine show of bearing & arms of company 7 also stores. Company employed on guards & fatigues & on company stores of bearing &c.	

Maj Hickin R.E.
21/3/19